GARDENING FROM THE HEART

Why Gardeners Garden

The seat of the soul is there,
where the outer and inner worlds meet.

NOVALIS

GARDENING FROM THE HEART

Why Gardeners Garden

by Carol Olwell

ANTELOPE ISLAND PRESS
1990

ISBN:0-917946-05-7 paperback edition
ISBN:0-917946-04-9 hardbound edition

Library of Congress Cataloging-In-Publication Data

Olwell, Carol, 1944-
    Gardening from the heart.

    1. Gardening—United States. 2. Gardeners—United
States—Interviews. I. Title.
SB455.049   1990   635   90-80777
ISBN 0-917946-04-9
ISBN 0-917946-05-7 (pbk.)

Designed by Hal Hershey and Carol Olwell
Typeset in Palatino and Goudy Old Style
Manufactured in Hong Kong by Dai Nippon Printing Co.

The quote on page 3 is from Joseph Campbell's *The Inner Reaches of Outer Space: Metaphor as Myth and as Religion*, (New York: Alfred Van Der Marck Editions, 1985), p.31.

Front cover: One of Marcia Donahue's sculptures, the goddess Daphne with spectacles, surrounded by bowling balls, a granite sculpture, and a pippin apple tree decked with tea cups.

Back cover: Close-up of another of Marcia Donahue's wooden sculptures in her backyard garden in Berkeley, California.

Published by Antelope Island Press
2406 McKinley Avenue
Berkeley, California 94703

To the memory of my grandmother

Lillian Riser Dooly

1893-1986

and

to all those individuals,

adults and children alike,

who care about, and are trying to take care of

the earth.

This stone sculpture, carved by Marcia Donahue, nestles in her backyard garden in Berkeley, California. To me it expresses the satisfaction and happiness that can come from gardening, and also my own feelings about working with the people acknowledged below.

Acknowledgments

I AM deeply grateful to all the gardeners I interviewed, and to all the gardeners whose interviews are included in this book. Meeting them was an honor, an inspiration, and a delight.

My thanks also go to the gardening editors of newspapers and agricultural extension division agents too numerous to mention individually who helped me locate these people.

I owe a particular debt of thanks to Lawrie Mott, Karen Snyder, and Sierra Club Books; to the Rachel Carson Council; to Marty

Strange, Liz Krupicka, and Dan Looker of The Center for Rural Affairs; and to Mary O'Brien of the *Journal of Pesticide Reform* for their willingness to share the results of their own pesticide research.

In addition, I would like to thank the Environmental Protection Agency for information on the environmental effects of pesticides, and also those who wrote and passed the Freedom of Information Act, making this information available to the public.

Typing is difficult for me, as I am dyslexic. I never would have been able to do this project without my personal computer and WordPerfect®. My thanks go to their developers for enabling this book to be completed within a reasonable amount of time, with a minimum amount of anguish.

I owe a special debt of thanks to the following people:

Marcia Donahue, for her encouragement in this project's early stages, for the inspiration that her garden was to me, and for her patience while I took *so* many photographs;

Ted Kipping, for his generous support and help in locating other gardening crazies;

Nina Feldman of Nina Feldman, Inc., and Ken Kegan of A Micro Assist, for their excellent transcriptions of the interviews;

Anne Edelstein, for being an author's dream of an agent; Cathy Luchetti, for her editorial help at the beginning of this project, and Ellen Dietschy, for her editorial help at the end;

Lynda Preston, for her suggestions, editorial skill, and organizational abilities which contributed immeasurably to this project;

Hal Hershey, for his talent and knowledge, and for his careful shepherding of this book's design and production;

My other friends, for their support and encouragement, and in particular Tobey Hiller and Phillip Ziegler, master gardeners of souls.

My last but most important thanks go to Ruthanne Lum McCunn, who believed in this book when even I was tempted to give up. Her steady encouragement, excellent suggestions, and unfailing support brought it to life.

TABLE OF CONTENTS

The toys of Kirk Kipping, left behind after a day of play in Ted and Pat Kipping's garden.

Introduction

THE SEEDS for a love of gardening are planted in many of us when we are children. I know it was so for me. In the 1950s, my maternal grandparents built a home in what we then called "the country," a rural area near Murray, Utah, about half an hour's drive south from Salt Lake City. For years it had been my grandfather's dream to design and build a house; my grandmother's dream was to have a larger garden. They purchased eleven acres, bounded on two sides by beautiful old trees that screened out nearby neighbors. Little Cottonwood Creek ran through their property, creating a refuge for wildlife and for us grand-children. The happiest moments of my childhood were spent there.

Today, Murray is simply one more faceless and somewhat ugly suburb, and my grandparents' entire neighborhood, including their eleven acres, has been paved over and plastered with wall-to-wall housing, or so I have been told by relatives. I have not had the heart to go back. In my memory, "the country" remains what I experienced in my youth—sunlit fields and inviting woods, the smell of the earth on a hot afternoon, birds singing, bees buzzing, and leaves rustling in the wind.

I can close my eyes and see my grandfather on his tractor out in the alfalfa field, and my grandmother on her knees in the garden. Although they grew vegetables for their own use and had a few fruit trees as well, flowers were my grandmother's favorites. She had a shoe box full of first-place and sweepstake ribbons her flowers had won at county and state fairs.

For many years, friends in a garden club, seed packets, and seed catalogs were her only sources of gardening information. Her garden was filled with annuals she grew from seed, not only because that was more economical, but also because there were no real nurseries in Murray then. There were no rare or exotic plants; instead her garden was full of common flowers that were very dear friends. Irises and gladioluses were found in abundance, while petunias, zinnias, salpiglossis, and cosmos were invited back year after year.

My sister, cousin, and I spent much of our time playing down by the creek. As sunlight filtered through the trees, we would jump from rock to rock, wade in the water, search for frogs and snakes and

Sign on the root cellar-guest house which overlooks Debbie and Jim Carlson's garden near Cooper Landing, Alaska.

bugs, and launch little boats of twigs and leaves that disappeared downstream. As I recall, we were never asked to help in the garden, and we probably didn't volunteer. So I didn't acquire any skills or knowledge about gardening from my grandmother. What I did absorb, as leaves absorb sunlight, was the sense that the earth was a truly beautiful and vibrant place, and that it deserved to be loved.

I didn't have the opportunity to have my own garden until almost thirty years later. What followed were a few years of very hard work that yielded very poor results. My soil was so alkaline that white bands of alkali salts would appear on the ground after each rain. Not even synthetic fertilizers could help; the soil had to be extensively treated with manure, organic waste materials, and other amendments first. I learned by necessity the organic dictum "Feed the soil, not the plant."

I am embarrassed to admit that when I started to garden, I didn't pay enough attention to the fact that different plants had different needs. Painful mistakes taught me that each little plant has its own requirements and rhythms, and that the task in gardening is somehow like an orchestra conductor's—being tuned to the whole moving through time, yet still being sensitive and responsive to each contributing member.

In talking with gardening friends, I began to realize the feelings I had about gardening were often quite different from theirs, and that people gardened out of needs that were largely unidentified and unexpressed. I looked for information about this in gardening literature. Garden design books, plant encyclopedias, and how-to books abound, but there is surprisingly little about *why* we garden.

I feel it is an important question because gardening is hard work. In our society it is work which has low social status and often brings limited, if any, financial reward. Yet millions of people do this hard work year after year, so the rewards, pleasures, and satisfactions have to come from somewhere else, from somewhere inside. Exploring that territory is what *Gardening from the Heart* is about.

I mentioned this idea to Keeyla Meadows, a gifted horticulturist. She told me about Marcia Donahue's garden, and when I went over to see it, this book was born. Photographs from Marcia's garden appear throughout the book because they exemplify its theme so well: as each person's garden is different, so too are the thoughts and feelings that produced it.

I wanted to interview people gardening in different areas and chose the geographical territory of the West because it offered the greatest diversity of soils and climates—from deserts to alpine meadows. The gardeners, however, come from all over the country, and some of them have even gardened in other parts of the world. I found these people by writing to gardening editors of newspapers and agricultural extension divisions, and by asking everyone I knew about friends or acquaintances who were gardening "nuts."

I looked for people who had a genuine interest in plants and trees, and who did all, or almost all in the case of older folks, of their own gardening work. Books already abound on estate gardens or those done in association with landscape crews; I was interested in gardens created by the gardener's own hands.

I wanted a wide variety of gardeners and gardens to begin to reflect the broad scope of thought and feeling in the gardening community. The people included in this book, however, are not representative of any area or line of work. They spoke only for themselves, and expressed views that were current at the time of the interview. Feelings and thoughts about everything, including gardening, change.

I taped every interview, and, on the same day as the interview, took photographs of the gardener and his or her garden. Each tape was transcribed and a statement drawn up of the gardener's views, using his or her words but my organization of our conversation. This statement was checked by the gardener for accuracy, and then underwent final editing.

It has been very difficult to find words for what happens between people and their gardens. I had hoped others would find it easier, but it was as hard for them as it was for me. It's like trying to tell someone you love why you love them. Indeed, I feel many of us experience a kind of personal love for our gardens. As Peter Levi put it: "There is something deeply erotic in the relationship of person and place; it includes endless exploration and happy repetition and silent familiarity; smell, sight, taste, touch, and hearing call it to life. I think it is literally too deep to be expressed in words, except sideways or casually, in the course of saying something else."[*]

To me gardening is, at the deepest levels, a metaphor for life itself. Perhaps that is why metaphors relating to gardening abound in our language: we "cultivate" friendships, "dig in" to get things done, "plant" ideas in "fertile ground," "put down roots," "weed out" things we don't want, "transplant" organs, or note someone is in "the bloom" of youth. To paraphrase Ecclesiastes, to everything there is a season, and a time to every purpose under the heavens. A time to be born and a time to die; times to sow and times to reap; times to tend carefully and times to painfully lop off. Times of rapid growth and times of almost imperceptible change. If the season or timing is missed, the consequences are irrevocable. I think that is part of why gardening can be so interesting, comforting, heartening, and heartbreaking, as well.

People have many different feelings about and motivations for gardening. In order to focus them, I have created four sections and somewhat arbitrarily divided gardeners among them, knowing that some people could have been included in every category. "The Garden as Paradise" deals with people who garden primarily to create a place of beauty, and who enjoy simply being with plants. In "The Garden as Provider" are people who earn their living growing food, or whose gardens are primarily food-producing. "The Garden as Teacher" deals with people who have discovered important things

[*] Peter Levi, "Knowing a Place," *Second Nature*, ed., Richard Mabey (London: Jonathan Cape, 1984), p. 42.

about themselves and life through gardening. "The Garden as Healer" deals with people who have experienced a healing of themselves and others through gardening, and who see it as one avenue of healing our society and the earth.

During the course of my interviews, I was surprised to find that many gardeners did not know how widespread and serious the problems of pesticide and environmental poisoning are, both nationally and internationally. Because these issues *are* so important, and because information on them is often very hard to find, I have included related material in the Appendix for readers who would like to inform themselves further. Also in the Appendix is a glossary of horticultural terms mentioned in the text.

Gardeners, like farmers, have traditionally been caretakers of the earth. They have been deeply, intimately involved with preserving its productivity, vitality, and beauty. A number of the people I interviewed seemed to be caretakers in this ancient tradition. They reminded me of candles flickering in the dark, lone individuals trying to do their best in a world preoccupied with other and often diametrically opposed values.

Meeting them gave me the feeling I had been introduced to a vast yet almost invisible network of support for the earth. These were individuals who never make the evening news or are widely acknowledged for their efforts, but who, day in and day out, go about the work they know is important to do.

Meeting them inspired me. They brought to mind something Buckminster Fuller often said: "On personal integrity hangs humanity's fate." He stressed that our lives and the viability of our planet cannot be saved from nuclear war, overpopulation, the decline of biological diversity, or the other global problems we face by the intercession of governments, businesses, or charismatic political and religious leaders. Our survival depends on the integrity of each individual, acting upon those larger powers and/or acting alone, exercising her or his own intelligence, initiative, competence, compassion, unselfishness, and love.

The earth is indeed a "Garden of Eden" in the vast expanse of space. It is the ground, quite literally, from which we draw our being. From it we receive everything—every breath we take, every morsel of food we eat, every thing we touch.

It deserves far better than the thoughtless use and selfish abuse that we of the twentieth century have been inflicting upon it. It deserves our deepest love, our thoughtful care, our comprehensive study, our sensitive restraint. Before it is too late, we must find ways of restoring to the earth the health and loveliness that come to it naturally, if given half a chance. One good place for the individual to begin is in a community garden, or in his or her own yard.

Hmong gardener watering her plot at the Unitarian Community Garden in Fresno, California.

The Garden as Paradise

Mary Kenady in her garden near Seattle, Washington.

Mary Kenady
GARDENING FOR BEAUTY

Mary Kenady and her husband, Reid, purchased ten acres outside of Duval, Washington, moving there in 1972 with their two daughters. On the fringe of the "back to the land" movement, they built their own home and also started a "minifarm" that included sheep, a goat, a horse, chickens, ducks, peacocks, geese, and the usual dogs and cats. Working full time, they commuted fifty miles round trip per day; Reid was teaching forestry at the University of Washington and Mary was a journalist for a local newspaper. After a few years the farm was just too much work; they decided to garden instead. So they "sold the horse, ate the lambs, gave away the geese, ducks, and goat, and found out that peacocks were delicious, too."

I read somewhere—or maybe it was Mark Twain who said—that gardening is what people take up when they find they can't change anyone else. I don't know if that is so. Maybe people garden out of a great love of doing something with living things. Maybe it's just a peaceful, tranquil thing to do.

I categorize gardeners in two ways. They are either natural gardeners who start paying attention to plants almost by instinct, while they are youngsters, or they migrate through various interests and come to gardening sometime during their mid-life. I'm of the latter variety. As a child in Iowa I always helped my parents in their vegetable garden, and I've puttered in gardens of one sort or another all my adult life. But I think being avid is just coming to me now.

My husband and I have always been outdoors people; all our camping and hiking trips were centered around my seeing unusual things in bloom in their natural habitat. I know birders who see almost nothing but birds when they go out in the country. I am a "planter" who sees nothing but plants.

Gardening is just an imitation of the delight I feel to discover a calochortus lily or some lewisia in the grass on the east side of our mountains. It was my love of the natural world that originally drew me into gardening, and when I go to a garden I always look for natural places, the places where I might find some little wildflowers hidden, or what's just volunteered itself somewhere. I think that is the most exciting thing to me.

In the beginning I didn't have an aesthetic approach to gardening, except for planting borders of annuals for color and bouquets. Instead, I just tried to recreate all of the natural world in my garden, no order or method involved. I wanted to grow everything in the Northwest native plant world, all the wildflowers and native plants that I loved. I studied the taxonomy of plants so that I knew what was what, and where it would grow. I collected seed and sometimes whole plants if they were in abundance.

A few things were spectacular successes, but most were not. What I really love most are alpines, and it isn't easy creating a natural environment for an alpine or semi-arid kind of plant a few hundred feet above sea level; those plants like to be frozen and covered up with snow in the winter. The plants native to this area are much more vigorous, and buttercups overtook the beds almost overnight.

In this country, if you leave an open meadow alone, it will be covered with blackberry bushes and alder trees as soon as you turn your back. So we gave up on the native and alpine plants, and have become much more interested in gardening as an art. We now see the fields in front of our house as opportunities for building large island beds of perennials, shrubs, and small trees. We've put in a pond because we get a lot of migrating waterfowl through here in the spring and fall. We'd like to make the whole place accessible with easy walking trails. Even though we have been working on this place since 1972, we still have a lot of dreams for our garden, and don't have enough time left in our lives for all the things we want to do.

I've experienced an evolution of ideas in gardening. I suppose everyone does. I know I have changed my gardening approaches, and why I garden as well. For a long time, as I gardened I would have big internal arguments with people and work out my sense of personal injustices, slights, regrets, and disagreements with relatives and friends. I realized a year or two ago that I was no longer doing that. There is a kind of peaceful hum going on inside instead, with only a little nagging imp off in the corner telling me that I'm not

A rustic arbor shelters a pond and bench for quiet moments in the garden, while through the arbor is the vegetable garden.

doing enough, and that I need to hurry up and finish this job because there are a dozen more that need attention.

So I was gardening, in part, to maintain my mental health; it was better than going to a psychiatrist, and a lot cheaper. I suppose I still garden for my mental health, but I am in remission right now. I have a more urgent sense of creation, of making something, of working with nature to achieve a compromise between us which will satisfy both. I am much more purposeful. I want to learn everything there is to know, an impossibility, of course, so that I can apply it here and as soon as possible. It's a mission.

What I enjoy most about gardening has changed, too. There was a time when my favorite thing was to come out of the garden with a basket full of vegetables just overflowing with wonderful things. It was a wonderful feeling and a great reward for all that work, and being able to give it away was part of it too.

Now I'm much more interested in the aesthetics of gardening. I think I do it for beauty. I am in search of absolute beauty. I have in my mind this vision, a composite of every alpine meadow I've ever walked through; small groves of trees, tight clumps of shrubs, acres of varied colors of flowers, a perfect pool, a perfect meandering stream. What could be more beautiful? It sounds trite to say I am in search of absolute beauty, but I can't express my love of gardening in any other way. It is a quest for a way to express an internal vision externally with a community of living things.

I took the Master Gardener course through the state and county extension service, and have belonged to garden groups in the past. But to be truthful, I'm not a big joiner. I like to do things by myself and to learn things on my own. Lately, I have joined a very active regional gardening group because I respect the knowledge and dedication of the people in it. I know I can learn from them, and I hope I can contribute something as well. My experience in the past with gardening groups hasn't always been good. In some garden clubs there can be a sort of rigid hierarchy, full of things that you do and don't do. I haven't liked how competitive and aggressive some ornamental gardeners can be: the one-upmanship, name dropping, social stratification, and control.

Why this should be true I haven't figured out, because certainly it isn't true among vegetable gardeners. When interviewing them for a book I did on vegetable gardening in the Pacific Northwest, I found that they are, on the whole, some of the most generous and helpful people alive. They love to share their produce and their knowledge;

A view of Mary and Reid Kenady's garden, surrounded by the forest they intend to protect.

they're practical and down-to-earth in every sense. In my opinion, in gardening there is room for every shade of honest opinion and every single person who wants to take part in the work and the reward.

Even our dachshund likes to garden. Our rhododendron bed often gets weedy over winter, and when we're working there in the spring, she'll come down with us because she loves to get out and do something. She'll bark and get all excited and grab weeds in her mouth and pull them up. She does this as long as we're doing it. She has infinite energy, and seems almost angry about the whole thing, as if she has a personal hatred for those weeds. She thinks she's helping, and she is to a certain extent.

But if she gets into a place where there are small plants we want to keep, she tends to chop them off too; then we have to be stern and order her out of the garden. She doesn't like that. Our Doberman tends to stay out of the garden if you tell her to, except for the occasional great flying leaps she takes right through the middle of my raised beds.

My husband helps me a lot in the garden. He does an incredible amount—all of the heavy lifting and hauling, and a lot of pruning. I help him, too, in his business, which is giving training courses in fire control for foresters.

We both have very deep feelings for trees. I am literally in pain when I see large trees cut. I believe there should be a federal law that any tree over a certain age or circumference must be protected and that a permit must be issued to cut it. Trees of a hundred years or more should be given respect and protection. Yes, they sometimes get rotten, and yes, they blow down and break off. Analogous things happen to us with age. They should be allowed to exist simply because the presence of trees much older than any human being alive is a humbling thing. They connect us with the past. Like the great old cathedrals of Europe, they stand as a reminder that we aren't the first, nor with some luck, the last.

We have, as a civilization, come so far as to offer certain protections to most mammals for at least part of the time. We acknowledge that they suffer pain and have certain rights to life. We haven't come to the point where we do the same for the plant world. Now I don't think I'm a sentimentalist, and I do acknowledge that we must kill daily to live. And I don't hear carrots screaming when I pull them up and eat them alive. But I do insist that it *is* killing and should be called that, not some euphemistic thing like "utilization of our natural resources."

I think I've learned over the years, sort of subconsciously, my connection with the earth in gardening. I feel a part of all this in no way that I can explain. I like best to be outside. I feel part of something very much bigger, something that feels right. In spite of all the really terrible things going on in the world, it is still possible to feel optimistic in the garden. It's partly a religious experience in a way to me, to feel connected with the earth, with time, and with the cycles of life.

*Loie Benedict surrounded by some of the foxglove (*Digitalis purpurea*) and campanulas (*Campanula latifolia*) found in profusion in her June garden.*

Loie Benedict
BLOOMING IN RETIREMENT

Many people look forward to retirement as an opportunity to garden intensively. For Loie Benedict, the chance came even later than that. She retired in 1969 to care for her ailing husband. He died in 1975, and at sixty-eight, when many people are winding down their gardening commitments, she began to garden full-time. Since then she has created a garden in Auburn, Washington, that is exceptional for its beauty and variety of rare plants, but perhaps her greatest pleasure is sharing her love of plants with a wide circle of gardening friends.

Actually, I never really spent a lot of time planning the garden. It just grew. But there are a lot of people in my garden; everybody's here in the form of some kind of plant that they gave to me. So my garden is filled with close friends and thought and study and associations, and I think about them as I work.

Everything just sort of goes together. To me, it's not a this or a that; I see it all as a whole. It's the same when I think about the people in my garden—their thoughts, the kind of things they like, the differences between them, you know, the way a garden reflects a personality, and no two are alike. I don't dissect it or think about things separately so much as I have a kind of feeling for the total.

I've always been interested in plants, ever since I was a child. A flower then was *something*, almost a mystical experience. I studied botany at the University of Washington, because I've always tried to find out all I can about something when I'm interested in it. Even when I was not actively gardening, I was always interested in everything about plants and flowers, and had garden magazines and garden books.

I started out with a vegetable garden, and even had corn growing. Then I discovered it was almost more work and more expensive to grow vegetables than to buy them, and that the ones I grew were not as good as those I could buy. So gradually the flowers crept in until finally the vegetables just went elsewhere.

I've always loved trees, too. I was born here in Washington, and spent a lot of my childhood in the woods. This is a wonderful country for trees. My father and brothers were loggers. Incidentally, my father logged the land about a mile diagonally from here, and I used to come up here with him. Did I think I'd ever be living within spitting distance of that place? No, I didn't!

I've had a checkered career. I left the University in my junior year because I didn't know what I was going to school for. I had to support myself entirely and pay for school too, and it seemed too expensive. For twenty years I did all sorts of different things, including working and getting married and living in California. And then my husband and I came back to Washington at the beginning of the Second World War, and he got a steady job. That was wonderful, you know, for the Depression was something we went through, too.

My husband worked for the government most of our married life. He was interested in writing and reading, and although he was not a plant person, he was indulgent and would screen dirt for me and take me places to see gardens before I learned how to drive,

Loie has combined hardy ferns, grasses, wildflowers, and herbaceous perennials for a long season of bloom.

when I was about fifty. He didn't interfere with my desire to acquire plants, and he even liked one or two of them. Agapanthus was one thing he liked.

We moved here in the spring of 1942; there were only two other houses on this road. Our ground sloped and was mostly brush, and there were woods all around. I didn't have to work at that time, and I would be home maybe two or three weeks at a time without anybody coming by, just my husband coming and going from work. I didn't drive or have a car, so I really lived right here.

That was the time when I did the hard work of clearing the blackberry vines and de-rocking, and I suppose planning or hoping, because we didn't have the money to buy anything much for the garden. But I was happy. We used the first sixty dollars we could spare to hire a bulldozer for one day to clear the fallen trees and stumps and ferns that were higher than your head.

For years it became just a field of grass because all that hard work of clearing the land had taken a toll on my back and legs. I had to have spinal surgery, and didn't know if I was going to be able to walk again. When I was lying in bed before the surgery, a friend of mine came over from Bremerton and brought me a shovel. It was a nice shovel, not a great big one, but a good-sized one. He stood it in the corner of the bedroom and said, "Now, get ready to use this shovel!" And you know, now I've got it so worn down that it is square on the ends.

As I recovered from the surgery, I had a feeling of new life, as if I'd been given a chance to do something, *really* do something. I was so happy to be able to get up and walk, and even though I couldn't do much for a year or so, I had a lot of time for thinking; at forty-eight I decided to become an occupational therapist. I had to go back to school to get a degree, and did my affiliations in Los Angeles, Denver, and the University of Oregon Medical School. I was a psychiatric occupational therapist until I retired in 1969 to care for my husband who was ill.

After he died, I hired a couple of boys to help me break up the sod, and we created the conditions for plants to grow. Since that time I've spent from six to ten hours a day out in the garden with a wheelbarrow and shovel. I get up, fix a simple breakfast, and often don't come in again until eight or nine o'clock at night. I never come in and eat lunch. I have a very large garden to take care of; it is about two acres, and I do almost all of it myself. It is a lot of planting and tending and watering. Maybe two days a month I have some help, and during the summer I hire a high school boy to mow the grass.

There are so many remarkable plants. I want to see all kinds, to take as many plants as I can through a cycle of growth and bloom while I'm still able. It worries me when I'm not taking good care of the plants; they are so generous with their rewards for any care you give them.

Gardening isn't static. It's different all the time. Everything is constantly changing — the size of the plant, the season. You can even juggle things about somewhat, although I'm not good at the pruning and the juggling because I hate to destroy anything that is living and growing. I've always had a respect for life.

For the last six or seven years I've supplied plants for the plant sale at the South King County Arboretum; they send a potting group over here two or three times a year, and we dig truckloads out of the yard. I go over to the sale and answer a lot of questions. That's fun, and I've made good friends that way, too.

The friends that I have are very interested in plants. They go abroad and get seeds from other countries, and we swap around. It's a regular exchange. I have joined a few plant groups and made some new friends. We have some wonderful times in the garden. But I wish that I had a bit more energy. I'm in my early eighties—and I'm running out of steam.

When the head of the Buchardt Gardens came here on a visit, even he asked for some seeds. A friend of mine who was at the Chelsea Flower Show in England brought me back Alan Bloom's current catalog, and I was amazed at how many of his very famous plants I have. Most of them have come from friends who've brought them from England or abroad, or I've bought the seeds through seed exchanges of the Hardy Plant Society or the Rock Garden Society. I do enjoy the study weekends of both societies, where we have lectures and garden visits. I've really enjoyed learning about plants; it's something in the genes, I guess.

Alan Bloom was at one of those study weekends when I did a small bit on the program. Afterwards the tour came here, and of course he came, too. But many people come to visit my garden; a group will be coming soon from the Seattle Arboretum. I gave a talk during their class on perennials and took from my garden just a collection of things that were in bloom at the time. Most of the plants were foreign to them, and they were so excited they wanted to come and see the garden. They'll bring a picnic, and we'll have fun.

When my husband and I first moved here, the house was just one room, and we worked on it a lot just to make it livable. At the time we built these additions, the garden had begun and I planned the shape of the house so that the light would be right and the planting could go along with it. I have a greenhouse area that wraps around most of the house and becomes a covered garden; in the wintertime when you look out the windows you see flowers. It is waist high so I can tend it without bending over because my back is giving out. For me, the house has always seemed an adjunct to the garden, not the other way around. My house will tell you where I spend my time.

It has only been within the last five years that all the houses around me have been built, and all of the people have moved in. For years and years, deer were regular visitors; one or two have come in through the woods only twice this summer. For about fifteen years, I fed a whole tribe of raccoons on the porch. They would get up on the windowsill because they knew where I sat, and we'd play patty-cake through the window. But the whole tribe must have been wiped out, for I don't see them any more — too many people, too many dogs, too much killing going on.

I like to create things that are beautiful. I think it comes out of my childhood, which was so barren. I sewed as a child and later painted and learned to weave. I always wanted to create something, to make things look nice. My mother had twelve children and we were very poor; it was a real problem just to keep everything together. I was the oldest girl, so, from the time I was five years old, I got to be nursemaid. I wore out all my maternal instincts before I was old enough to go to school. In many ways my plants seem to me like my younger brothers and sisters.

I worked my way through school taking care of other people's children, and worked with children when I became a psychiatric occupational therapist. I suppose I empathize with kids because we didn't have a very easy time of it. Growing up and learning about life and being able to meet the challenges and the threats and the stress are very hard on people all of their lives.

I think childhood, if it isn't invaded by too many adult require-ments, is a different world to live in. There is curiosity and meeting something for the first time, you don't have it categorized or in a slot. It's an experience on its own. You don't see it as an object, you relate to it as part of yourself. The philosophers talk about this being a mystical experience, but I think it's an uncontaminated relationship that comes directly when you are a part of what you see.

As a child, I remember the experience not of looking at some-thing but of *being* what I was seeing. It happened two or three times, and when I learned to reason, I thought about it. By that time, of course, I had outgrown that state. But in about 1979, a friend took me to see a dahlia farm he was interested in. It was a hot day, the dahlias were in bloom, and I was standing in his shadow because he was tall. I turned to see an enormous, dark, almost blood-red dahlia. I don't know where I was, but I was not there for a little bit. My friend looked at me and said, "What happened?" I said, "I was the dahlia." It's not something you can explain or tell about. You can just say that it happened. A couple of times since then it has happened. The first daffodils of spring will often clue me in to that other kind of existence where I'm not separated.

I garden with back pain much of the time because I've had back pain most of my life. I think, because of the way I was raised—which was more or less left to grow up without a lot of supervision—that I have a pretty realistic sense. What is, is. So working while I'm in pain isn't being a martyr, it is just knowing this is the way *it is*.

If you're going to do something, you undertake an obligation either to the material or to someone else. The nice thing about a garden is that you're just doing it for your *own* pleasure. And when I get tired and I'm not getting things done, I tell myself, "After all, I started this for my own pleasure!"

But I garden for the pleasure of the plants as well. I need them, but they need me too. I have a respect and regard for them, and I'm aware of their different personalities and their requirements. They're living things, beautiful in themselves, and I like to help them grow. I don't talk to my plants, but I do sense a relationship. After all, don't we all have the same DNA? But I don't deal with them on human terms. To me that is imposing your own needs on the plant. The plant is its own being, and I am my own being.

My father cleared land all his life. I always remember him cutting trees and brush and plowing and planting. I suppose that's

Loie's garden includes rhododendrons, azaleas, magnolias, hybrid lilacs, kalmia, hypericums, clematis, cornus, sequoia, roses, pines, and maples, to name only a few.

33

part of why I like most to get the ground ready. That is really stimulating, and where the real change comes in. The rocks go out and the ground is made fertile. Then I'm faced with "What am I going to plant here?" and I have to start thinking, I have to shift gears entirely. When I'm doing something physical, I think I'm more aware of what is going on. My mind is working, but in a different way than when I'm trying to figure something out.

A friend told one of her friends that he had to see my garden because, "It was just like this lady threw things about and said, 'Let there be flowers.' " Now and then I get into the business about colors and the blooming season and heights, but what I've tended to do in the past is not spend too much time on that. I've got these plants, I've got this space, and I put them in where they will do well.

Some of my friends' gardens are very much under control. No plant can be more than a certain height or go farther than a limited area. I'm simply interested in helping a plant make its own way in the world, as it were. Plants, if they're happy where they are, get bigger and bigger within their capacity to grow, and like people, compete for space. When that happens I try to move the plant, to give it space somehow. That means, of course, eventually the whole world would be a garden because you'd need space and space and space, and that wouldn't be so bad.

Fragrance is one of the most important things in gardening. Fragrance can sell a plant to me even if not much else is there. When I'm weeding, I know what I'm pulling up because I can smell the bruised juice and remember which smell goes with which plant.

I have a tremendous compost pit down below, which I've been building over the years and am now harvesting. I use that with a bale of peat moss and a little steer manure for some things because my soil doesn't have much humus in it. I sometimes use both steer manure and commercial fertilizer because this hill's soil is gravelly; that's what forest soil is, a rocky soil. When people say, "Oh, you don't have any rocks," I take them to see my tons and tons of rock walls and things I've hauled out over the years.

But plants grow very well here, so I've never had the pH of the soil tested. I try something; if it doesn't work, I try something else. I don't use herbicides or sprays because if I put anything on the ground here, with its slope, it would soon be down in the river. The only poisons I use are the powdered slug bait and Deadline.

If I have a favorite time of year, I think it is fall. Perhaps it is the colors, or the crisp mornings and the bright sunshine. The air feels different. You're through the rush of summer and there is the sense of everything calming down. I always liked to pick fruit. I don't do much of it any more because ladder work is out of the question, but I used to love to climb up in the branches and pick apples and cherries.

I think as you get older your evaluation, your sense of what's important, changes. There are very few things that are really important when you get old. Objects and ideas and a variety of relationships continue to be interesting, but they're less necessary. You don't identify in the same way with those things. You probably have a more complete sense of who you are and what your needs are, and you can scale down.

Actually, I think relationships are the most significant thing in life. I tell people, "I'm famous for my friends." I've met some wonderful people along the way. They've been very great influences—some of my teachers and two or three friends that popped up at the right time. I think we're very fortunate if that occurs. Many people never have that experience.

A friend of mine from Portland asked, "How do you ever manage?" I replied, "Well, it's from six to ten hours a day, eight days a week!" I sometimes think I'm a gardening fool, a fool to be working this hard at my age when my back hurts so much. It is getting to be a struggle now, the bending over and stooping and lifting.

But I can't stop. I'm addicted. When you have limited energy, you have to decide where you're going to put it because it runs out pretty quickly. Gardening isn't the only thing I'm interested in, but gardening and my friends are the things that I'm most willing to give myself and my energies to.

Marcia Donahue with a morning cup of tea, sitting next to a pot of Scirpus tabernaemontani zebrinus.

Marcia Donahue
A GARDENING ARTIST

To enter Marcia Donahue's garden in Berkeley, California, is to slip into a world full of mythological symbols and botanical delights. A former fiber artist, Marcia likes to create theme areas in her garden, and to combine odd plant forms, sculptures, and other objects she has made or scrounged from salvage yards, flea markets, and the dump. She calls herself a horticultural thrill seeker. Qualities of play, exploration, and delight are evident throughout her garden. Presiding over it is a painted statue of the goddess Flora, sitting atop an eleven-foot pillar, split and sprouting like a seed.

As a child I had a garden, just a little place where I would plant things I had rescued from the creek behind our house. A nursery close by would dump castoffs there. I'd save those little things and grow them. I really cared about that garden, to the point of dreaming about it sometimes. Then my life took lots of twists and turns, and I never had the place or the time to garden. Although I always loved plants and visited botanical gardens and arboretums, the opportunity to have a garden didn't come until five years ago, when my husband, Chris, and I finished putting a new foundation and roof on our house.

This was a little weed patch when I began. It had all the classic Berkeley banes: heavy clay soil, Bermuda grass, blackberries, and ivy. I started by just making a hill in the middle and worked out from there, winding a path around it with the cast-off bricks from the old foundation of our house.

Rich soil is important because I plant so closely. My soil is gorgeous now after double digging and putting in *tons* of organic matter. If we were to sell the house, for me the main selling point would be the good, fluffy soil. I use organic techniques because it appeals to me not to have poison in my own little place, although there are still all kinds of fungal diseases. Those damn roses just catch everything!

This garden has been planned in tiny little increments, and I'm constantly altering it. It was not primarily made to be pretty, but it is growing in a way that pleases me. It has a lot of emotional content, and a lot of it is deliberately composed: I put ribbons on the rose bushes when all their branches were bare—just a little something for those bare, bare twigs in the gaunt season.

I studied art as an undergraduate in Massachusetts and have a master's degree in textiles. The garden really grew out of my art work; they're very, very related. Instead of going down in the basement or up to the attic to make indoor stuff, I just went outside with my work. I've always been material oriented in my work, and now I have this material to compose with that just thrills me. You can't beat plants, soil, and space under the sky. They give you so much. They're so generous, so nice to collaborate with.

For some reason, the act of making things brings up heavy stuff for me. It just does. Working in the studio was sort of painful and lonely. In the garden it isn't that way; there's a lot of company out there among the plants and images. I realized when I was in the studio that part of what was painful, but absolutely necessary and to

The goddess Flora gazes down at the flowers and at blossoms made of plates, cups, and saucers. The steel cutout sculptures were made by Marcia's friend Mark Bulwinkle.

the point, was the idea of change. That nothing stays the same. And a lot of my work called up feelings of death or fossils or things that have changed.

I'm trying, as a transient form of life myself, to come to terms with living and dying and constant change. There is no security, or the only security is that things keep changing. In the garden, change seems so uncreepy, so wonderful at every stage. There is nothing more fluid than a garden. Nothing holds still out here!

Just as people rearrange their furniture, I like to keep changing things around in the garden, trying to keep current. I'm learning, my ideas change, and I feel I'm getting better at this. Many skills are involved: not only horticultural, or how to grow things, but also how to design and to express. I have garden mania to an advanced degree. I'm out there every morning. The intensity is building each year as I learn. I love it!

Sometimes when I am out in the garden, or in someone else's garden, I have the feeling of the skin being peeled away from my eyes. It's as if I'm seeing something for the first time, really seeing it. It's a feeling of a whole moment that just comes and fills me and buzzes me. It's being able to see with fresh eyes.

My husband, Chris, is a carpenter. When I need help, he is always right there. He's not wildly enthusiastic about what I do, but deep down, he's very supportive. He looks at my efforts when I point them out, and he enjoys people enjoying them. But he doesn't have a particular interest in plants, and he doesn't want to garden. My daughter is sixteen and doesn't garden either. She's touched by it, but not actively involved.

So, the garden is like my own room, like "a room of one's own." Here, I'm the boss and the chief admirer. It touches every part of my life. I've committed time and attention to it. I've let it take me over. Since I am only working part-time, I can concentrate and "go with the flow" of it. I feel blessed that I have the chance to do this because, in its way, this is a time-consuming and expensive passion. Gardening for me is really just thrilling. It engages me completely, in every sense. I even have come to love the sweaty hard work of it.

For me, the garden is a very extravagant place in all ways. I want everything. That's why it's so crowded! I have several themes running throughout the garden. The goddess is just one of them. I've been working on a goddess theme for a long time, even before I started gardening, so it's natural to bring that into the garden. One of the reasons for making these kinds of figures is to suggest the defense and protection some deity might provide in a world that is so painful. People making gardens create a kind of enclosure, a safe spot. I also suppose part of why I choose to make goddesses is just the desire to make sculptures that embody something important.

So I have been semi-intellectually looking around for gods and goddesses appropriate to the garden. The goddess Flora is a beautiful mythological image. She evokes for me sexuality and fecundity, from seed to fruit to compost; it's life, the whole thing. I love the figure of the Virgin Mary, the Madonna. I'm not Catholic, but she has always appealed to me, with her veil over her head and that embracing, streaming-out quality. So I have a few Marys in the garden, too.

There is also a Daphne-Apollo theme running throughout this garden. I started out with Daphne because she turned into a tree. When I was young, I was struck with the image of Daphne in the same way I was struck with the image of the Madonna. Daphne is so

Marcia's forty-seven by-sixty-foot backyard is densely planted. Here a Bourbon rose bush (Rosa Louise Odier) is flanked by Madonna figurines. Along the path a small bush is decked with peach-colored ribbons to cheer its spirit until spring.

ambiguous. She made choices and yet had things act upon her, too. I always wonder if she was glad Artemis turned her into a tree. Was it any better? As an image in the garden, she seemed so appropriate.

But the more I mess with it, the more I wonder what I'm messing with. I like the idea of woman resisting rape and finding refuge in the plant kingdom. That's a defense theme which tender little me requires! On the other hand, as a woman artist, I wonder what would happen if somehow, powerfully, she didn't resist. If there were some way she could join with Apollo, have his child, et cetera. I haven't thought it out all the way; I need to understand it more. Recently, for instance, I learned that Apollo was a patron god of art. I think that I'm just juggling a whole bunch of symbols, some of which I probably know inwardly and don't realize, and others which have to do with more than I might think!

I have, however, been playing with the Daphne-Apollo theme. In one area of the garden I have Daphne turning into a coral bark maple; in another area she becomes a stake to support floppy plants. The southern fence is a "hedge" made of big wooden comic strips

The unexpected greets the visitor at every turn. Forks, spoons, plates, and hair curlers sprout from the soil. Other photos of Marcia's garden are on the front and back covers, and on pages 9 and 233.

which depict the Daphne legend as if it had occurred in other times and places, rather than ancient Greece.

The Mars garden is a hill that says "Martian" in red theater marquee letters. It is where I plant things that are well defended, or look like they are from outer space, or are red. The best rose in my whole collection is planted on top of the Mars garden, a species rose from China with huge translucent red thorns. Its new canes, backlit by the morning light, are just as brilliant as the red backlit plastic. And what movement—it dances in the wind all day long. Vita Sackville-West had one planted near her writing tower so she could admire it.

I prefer uncommon plants, such as the *Tropaeolum tuberosum*, a form of nasturtium that has an edible tuber that was once a staple food of the ancient Peruvians. I also like to know about the historical background of the plants in my garden. I have an Eglantine rose, the kind Shakespeare wrote about, and a damask rose, *(Rosa damascena bifera)*, the rose that Homer and Ovid were talking about when they wrote "rose."

But I don't really do an organized search for a particular plant. Often I just stumble upon them: "Oh, there's a . . . ! I've always wanted a . . . !" Sometimes I don't even realize I have to have a plant until I see it; then I am just absolutely swept away. For some reason it appeals to me.

There are always limits, of course. Price is a part of it. But, one thing about the gardening world is although it's expensive as a hobby, it's possible. Each little chunk doesn't usually cost more than x amount of dollars. I've low budgeted all my life; just no money to speak of. And although I've really let myself, by hook or by crook, go gung-ho in the garden, I still take a very scrounging approach. I do start cuttings and exchange with other gardeners, and I do steal things from the landfill.

But this ongoing thing of taste, it is so extravagant and frivolous in one way and so to-the-point in another. I am very interested in watching what appeals to me. It seems that part of this process is finding oneself in the outside world. If something appeals, it's me. It is like the world is a mirror, and there I am in this form! For me, that's what matters. That's what tastes are, things that ring true to me. I'm not interested in the issue of "good taste." By paying attention to what appeals to me, I'm trying to find out what I like, and what I'm like.

When I was nine or ten, I had a strong desire to go down to the creek where we lived and dig out a little niche in the bank, to have this tiny shrine sort of place. In it I wanted to put a beautiful Madonna statue that I would buy at the dime store. I never did it, but I thought about it. It was embarrassing, and sort of taboo. At least in my family it would have been. To me, it was attractive in a way that was almost sexy because it was powerful and taboo.

I feel that finally I've granted that wish for myself. I get to do it, I'm doing it publicly all over the place, and I'm enjoying it with other people, too. I want my work and my life to be one whole, not compartmentalized. That's a conscious desire of mine, to have it really add up to a whole thing, a whole life.

I love having garden visitors. People laugh and get off on the place. It is so much nicer to show work there rather than in a gallery or even a living room. In the garden, people feel relaxed and receptive. They respond to the spirit of the place whether or not they know the myths. I have never heard, "What is this supposed to mean?" or "My kindergartner could do better." I have received warm and genuine thanks. Art has its difficulties as a way of relating to oneself and others. Having my garden become my art work really seems to get around some of that.

Bob Shepherd holding a branch of Eucalyptus nutans. *The feathery, green-gray native plant behind him is old-man sagebrush.*

Bob Shepherd
DESERT GARDENER

It is one thing to create a beautiful garden in rich soil and a temperate climate. It is quite another to create an outstanding garden in the desert. Although in their seventies, Bob and Olive Shepherd have done just that, transforming windswept dunes on a three-quarter acre lot in Santa Clara, Utah, into a refreshing oasis. Trees are the main points around which the landscape evolves; Bob has planted Arizona cypress, ruby-laced locusts, cork oaks, desert willows, and twenty-four varieties of eucalyptus, to name only a few. He even did most of the digging for a small swimming pool in which he cools off during the summer, because for more than four months of the year he and Olive garden in over one-hundred degree heat.

Why do I like to garden? Patterns are built bit by bit, and to find the beginning of my interest in gardening, I must go back to my early childhood. My mother was a neat, well-organized person who loved pretty things but never had many of them. Father was a capable, practical man who liked music and art and had some talent in both but never followed up on either. He was of an independent nature and preferred to be his own boss, so he became a traveling salesman. Mother had to find employment to feed the family.

We had three-quarters of an acre of ground that included fruit trees, a strawberry patch, a raspberry patch which I hated because I had to prune it, and a vegetable garden. We didn't have many flowers. Since both of my parents were away working, I was taught to cultivate, weed, and irrigate the garden, and I didn't like it.

As the eldest child I was given responsibility early. We had no close neighbors with children my age so I became a loner; drawing and painting entertained me. By the time I was six years old, I knew that I wanted to become an artist. I took all the art classes available in school. When time came for college, I opted for architecture because it involved creative design and would be financially more rewarding than painting. I loved architectural design but failed in engineering, so I went into architectural drafting instead.

I married Olive Fuller, my high school sweetheart, after seven years of courtship. That was in 1932, at the height of the Depression. I had worked for three firms that went bankrupt and had even lost a house that I had started to buy. When Olive's father offered me employment on the Fuller farm in return for our room and board if we should get married, I accepted the offer. I became a farmer for a couple of years until we were able to buy some land and start to build a house.

My mother, by then a widow, offered us two thousand dollars if we would include a bedroom and bath for her. That two thousand dollars built the whole house, because Olive and I did all the work by ourselves, except for hiring a plumber to caulk the cast-iron drain pipe for the sewer system.

When I drew the house plans, a landscape plan was part of the package. I was not afraid to dream big. On that two acres I planned and built an outdoor fireplace, archery range, horseshoe pits, badminton court, formal rose garden with a fountain in the center, a rock garden, a water lily pond with gold fish, as well as an orchard, chicken coop, and vegetable garden! We also had a swimming pool which I dug out and built myself. Our home became a showplace and was featured in a full-page article in the *Salt Lake Tribune*.

By now I was addicted to gardening. My local nurseryman became a very good friend and often gave me varieties of plants to try out. I loved landscaping; it seemed to be a marriage between painting and architecture, a living thing involving change as the plants mature. When I had everything set and growing well, I would come up with a better idea, and would start digging things up and transplanting them. One of the neighbors once commented, "You should have wheels on your plants because you're always moving them around."

I also discovered the excitement of gambling in gardening. There are so many variables. The weather may wipe out your latest project or give you lush growth. In spite of all of the reading and research you do and experience you gain, Mother Nature finally determines the outcome.

In 1953, I went to Los Angeles as a draftsman and later to do mural painting in the new Mormon Temple on Santa Monica Boulevard. I became so enamored with the tropical plants that grew there that I was able to convince my wife that we should sell our Salt Lake City home and build in the warm coastal area. I was tired of not being able to garden for six months of the year, and wanted a chance to grow all those tropical plants.

We built on an acre of ground in a walnut grove in Woodland Hills. It was the finest house that I've had, but the trouble was that I felt like I was caged, with all the big walnut trees around me. One winter we had a heavy frost which killed some of my trees and shrubs. I noticed that the gardens on the hillside didn't freeze because the cold air had settled in the valleys, so I looked around and found a lot on the top of a hill. We sold our nice home and bought two acres of hilltop with a magnificent view.

It was a little hilltop and a lot of slope in all directions. There was no level ground; we had to cut and fill to get enough level area to build on. The same thing applied for the garden areas. We had to construct paths and level off and terrace the planting areas. Olive and I did the work, and it was a lot of work.

But what a grand place it became! We combed the nurseries for exotic shrubs and trees. What a thrill it was for a couple born and raised in the temperate zone to enjoy year-round exotics such as gardenias, azaleas, camellias, and even orchids. And so many varieties of wonderful trees! We had a small vegetable garden and an orchard including citrus and avocado. I worked out an Italian garden adjacent to the dining room. We could look down and see the formal pattern with an elaborate fountain in the center. Down a little farther there was a desert garden with many varieties of cacti, aloes, agaves, and other succulents. There was also a very private and secluded meditation garden with a fountain surrounded by a circle of tall cypress trees. There was an entertainment center with a brick barbeque, a jogging circle, and a giant swing that swung out over the edge of the hillside. Children from all around the neighborhood used to come and ask, "Can we walk around on your paths?"

I sold that house to an actor, and he sold it a year later to someone else. About three years after that, I stopped by to see it. It was utter desolation. It was heartbreaking. They hadn't watered a thing. The azaleas, camellias, and gardenias around the house were all dead. The fountain had dried up and the cement had cracked. The trees were dying. They had been totally neglected. It looked like a horror movie, as if you'd made a setting for Dracula. I just shed tears.

Now I'm concerned about my present home and garden. I say, "Look, I've only got a few more years on earth here now, and what is going to happen to this? I hate to leave it to be destroyed. How can I be sure that somebody will take care of it?" I've asked my daughter who lives nearby what she would do if she had the home and she said, "We like to garden a little bit, but no, we wouldn't want to be saddled with your place." And my son is back in Chicago, so that wouldn't work. So I guess I'll just have to remain here on earth to take care of it.

Well anyway, I sometimes ask myself, "Why did I give all that beauty up to come to the hot dry desert area of southwestern Utah?" I must have been crazy. I didn't give it much thought at the time because I had already created three beautiful places. The smog, the fact that the area was no longer rural, and rising taxes made me decide that I could no longer afford to live there. I wanted to retire and to paint, so we looked for another place, sold our California home, and came here to start all over again. I've had to learn a whole new language of different plants and to find out what would do well. It has been a real challenge to garden in Santa Clara.

I guess I selected southwestern Utah because of the multitude of beautiful things to paint. Santa Clara is just five miles from Snow Canyon, a strikingly beautiful place, and within a radius of 150 miles are the Grand Canyon, Lake Powell, Zion Canyon, Cedar Breaks, and Bryce Canyon. What more could a landscape painter want?

*The desert plant area in Bob's backyard: the two tall trees in the rear are Nichol's willow-leaved peppermint (*Eucalyptus nicholii*) and cider gum (*Eucalyptus gunnii*); in the right foreground are a Joshua tree (*Yucca brevifolia*) and fig tree.*

We selected a lot with a beautiful view of the desert and red hills topped by blue Pine Valley Mountain. I hadn't planned on doing much gardening here, for these were to be my retirement years, and I wanted to be free to paint. So I bought only two lots to build on, and designed a red-tile-roofed Spanish home that I thought was compatible with the desert. I planned desert landscaping for the front of the house, but when one is in the desert, one seeks an oasis, so I planted green shade trees and lawn at the sides and back. Nothing is more refreshing in the desert than a pool of water, so a swimming pool was necessary. Then we had to have a vegetable garden and fruit trees and grapes, so I could see we needed more land. We bought a third lot to the north giving us three-fourths of an acre. Now I feel the need of still more land, and none is available.

The different areas of my garden are kind of like rooms in a house. I create an area, and another area, and the next area may be entirely different. I want to create a whole new picture, a new atmosphere. Yet there must be an overall relationship that ties the whole together. Trees are first; they are the big elements, and then other things fill around. Floral display is secondary with me. It's something like planning a painting: you plan your big areas first, and then start decorating your smaller ones.

The major part of my back lot is a desert garden. I have tried to preserve many of the native plants growing there naturally, such as the creosote bush, broomweed, little leaf ratany, Mormon tea, cheese bush, old-man sagebrush, cholla cactus, and others. I planned this area of the garden around these plants, and was soon out scouting for other interesting plants that were not growing on my property. Generally I have been quite successful in transplanting, but so far I have failed completely with Indian paintbrush and prickly poppy.

The soil and climate are difficult. The soil is sandy and alkaline, devoid of organic material. The summers are hot and dry and the

Cacti provide visual variety and a sculptural element in Bob's garden; their colors blend beautifully with the color of the soil.

A corner of Bob's ornamental garden. The evergreen tree on the far right is a Japanese black pine (Pinus thunbergiana), and next to it is a young pistachio tree (Pistacia vera). The gazebo gives refuge from the 115 degree heat.

winters are cool and dry. It's really a matter of learning how to use the miniclimates; there are so many around here that make a whale of a difference.

My garden is pretty much organic. I should give it more fertilizer mainly because it doesn't have a lot, but as I said, I'm experimenting to see what plants will make it within these conditions. If I feed them heavily, that doesn't prove anything. The things that are growing in the back of the yard are doing pretty well without fertilizer. All they get is a little bit of water. Some of the small trees and new shrubs I water by hand, but the big body of the garden gets watered about every three weeks by a set of sprinklers. It could survive without this, but it does better if it gets a drink once in a while.

I don't consider myself a very good gardener. The caring for plants—feeding them, spraying to take care of the diseases—is not my field particularly. It has to be done, but I'm not too knowledgeable about it. Designing is my expertise, and the main thing that I like about gardening. I love to create beauty, and landscaping is just another form of art.

One spring while visiting the local nursery, the owner asked if I wanted to plant a couple of eucalyptus trees that some young fellow had left, and he did not want to bother with them. I gladly accepted. Later that fall, a young man knocked at my door and asked if I had planted a couple of eucalyptus trees. I showed them to him, and he asked if I would like to try some more. I agreed so he left several with me. Thus began a very close friendship with Dale Rose, who at that time was attending college at UCLA. He is now a commercial grower with Southwest Plants, Inc., in Palmdale, California.

Dale continues to drop off plants for me to try. All my twenty-four varieties of eucalyptus came from him, and I have several still in cans as replacements, awaiting the demise of some that can't adjust to the area. I have six varieties of palm trees surviving the winters. It is difficult to add new trees and shrubs to an already landscaped area without destroying the design of it, so Dale has gotten me into a very interesting new hobby. Now my yard is changing from a landscaped area to an experimental garden. If one shrub or tree dies, I don't mind because it gives me room to plant another.

I think that the interesting thing about gardening is that it is an ongoing thing. You may have things looking nice for one year, and you've got it all planned out. In a year or two those trees and plants have grown. Their appearance has changed so you either have to prune them or relocate them and plant something else. If you choose your season, fall or spring, you can transplant quite well.

I'm out here in the garden in winter from about ten o'clock in the morning until three or four in the afternoon. In the summertime I'm working outside from about six o'clock until ten o'clock in the morning, and again from about six o'clock in the evening until dark.

Olive and I both enjoy gardening together, but Olive, the farmer's daughter, is the keeper of the vegetable garden and I, the artist, am free to do as I please with the rest of the yard. Neither of us will make any changes within our own areas without the approval of the other. So the garden is part of both of us.

So why do I garden? I love beauty. It brought me much satisfaction when some of the old-timers who used to herd cattle all over this area said, after seeing my garden, "We didn't know these plants were so beautiful. We used to just knock them down." As an artist it is my job to call attention to and preserve some of that beauty so that others may also enjoy it. Gardening is a joint activity for my wife and me, and I give it credit for keeping us healthy physically, mentally, and spiritually. Being close to nature is being close to God.

Sarah Nichols and Mrs. Jackson in Mrs. Jackson's backyard.

Sarah Nichols
NEIGHBOR EXTRAORDINAIRE

*Sarah Nichols has what she calls a "well-developed case of garden euphoria"
which has begun to transform her entire block in Berkeley, California. Feeling
the need for "just a bit more space to have a few more things," she made a
trade with her neighbor to the north, Mrs. Ida Jackson, who is 110 years old.
In return for being able to plant what she wanted, Sarah took down the fences
between them and has done all the clearing, soil amending, planting, and
watering for free. After a while, she made the same agreement with her
neighbor to the southeast. Recently another neighbor, Eloise, said "Anything
you want to do in my yard is okay by me!" and a small fruit orchard has been
the result.*

Sarah's home is a one-room-wide farmhouse brought down from the Berkeley hills in 1928. Her front yard supports a profusion of flowers from spring until autumn.

There was a large pine tree in Mrs. Jackson's backyard which her only son had planted when he was a little boy. Her son died as a young man, before he had any children, and then the pine tree died. When I moved here, it was a tall dead snag, and the wind kept breaking the limbs off. Our communication first started when I was able to convince her to cut it down, although she wanted a tall stump left there in his memory.

I discovered she was someone who loves and appreciates flowers. It was like two people who drive the same motorcycle, or love the same music; you suddenly have this same world and vocabulary. I started bringing her flowers on a regular basis. Then I took down the fence between us and slowly started clearing her yard out. Because of her age she hadn't been able to work in it for a number of years.

Sarah's backyard is small but densely planted and extends into the garden she planted for another neighbor.

It's like a marriage made in heaven, a kind of divine gift that I get more space to garden in, and she, in the last years of her life without having to make any effort, is surrounded by beauty. Just today she said, "You know, whenever I get lonely, I go outside and look at those flowers, and I realize that life is just too sweet to whine about."

All she has to do is tell me what she likes and, you know, it's there for her. She likes yellow flowers so I filled up her yard with yellow flowers. It absolutely thrills me that I'm making this woman so happy.

When I first started gardening in her yard, she'd say, "I like those calendulas, you really don't need to weed those." Now it is to the point where she trusts me enough, and there is so much for her to see, that she's just delighted with anything I do, which, in terms of my joy and love of gardening, is perfect for me. She's the ideal neighbor. My only concern is that when she dies, the next people to move in there are going to have a tremendous impact on my life. I only wish she were eighty years old.

She can't believe that I'm willing to do all this for free. When I cleared her yard out the first time she said, "Well, how much do I owe you?" This was when I was doing this kind of work professionally, getting sliding scale from ten to fifteen dollars an hour, and I said, "Oh, you don't have to worry about it." She said, "No, no, no, I insist. I really want to pay you." So I said, "Well, what have you got?" and she said, "Peppermints." Right now upstairs I have a big bag of peppermints.

It has taken her a while to trust me. She's very proud and has no interest in charity. And it has taken her a while to realize I really do like doing this, and part of the reason is that it makes her so happy. Really, the raison d'être of my garden right now is to make my cat and Mrs. Jackson happy. And in the meantime, there is all this other "fallout" for all the rest of us to enjoy.

My cat is quite remarkable in how she respects the garden. She follows all the paths and doesn't walk through the garden. It's really interesting how, when I "open up new territory" and put in a new path, she will follow that. It gives me joy to find the little nests where she sunbathes. Of course, after I create nice, fluffy, freshly turned earth, she likes to poop in it, but that's her only problem, and she doesn't do that a lot. She does it in the other yards that I tend.

I was fortunate in having a really wonderful childhood in Davenport, Iowa, and as I look back on it, the pleasant memories are sort of exemplified by plants. That's why there are plants I've just got to have. The first tree that I climbed was an ancient rosebud tree, so I planted a rosebud tree in Mrs. Jackson's yard. I have this romance for peonies and lots of other things that like colder weather. So in the winter I go to the liquor store and buy bags of ice and put them on top of my peony plants. I want to have that magic feeling in my garden that I had in childhood, that the world is really wondrous.

We lived on the Mississippi River, near ravines created by tributaries. The ravines couldn't be developed because they were steep, and because they were watersheds. We kids had fabulous trails through these ravines which ran like veins of wilderness through the entire town.

Our house had a garden that was at least fifty years old. It had the feel of a secret garden—totally overgrown, filled with irises. When my father died when I was eleven, the house was just filled with flowers, and that's what got me through the funeral.

I like to garden because it is an opportunity to be as egoless as possible. You have the chance to participate in a world that is so much larger than you, a world that is forever changing. I paint too, and yet gardening is not like painting, where you create a trophy that you put on the wall when you finish it.

To me, gardening is the highest form of human endeavor. Cultivating the earth is one thing that the other animals don't do. We have this ability to create all this beauty. It's amazing how, as the garden grows, it grows on you and with you. You end up being the human that's there to tend it.

In my garden I try to create a world that has its own life and vitality. I think I'm doing my best if my imprint is not overtly stated; Sarah Nichols is here and there is her touch, but the garden speaks for itself. All that I am, fortunately, is the human being that is caring for it, and has the passion to want a Tibetan lily in her yard.

Gardening for me is definitely a love affair, and I have new affairs all the time. This year it's lilies and rhododendrons. I truly get a relationship going with the plants. Plants I don't even like I feel badly about abandoning. That's one of the reasons I need to garden in my neighbors' yards—to have a place to put the plants that I don't want to live with any more.

I'll go through a period where I'm madly in love with the whole process. Then circumstances take me off, and I'm no longer able to participate with it intensely. And then, as I get back into it, I truly get this momentum going. Gardens have their own cycle of seasons, their own ebbs and flows, and I do, too. I go through periods when I am totally tired of the whole process, and when that happens, the garden ebbs.

Spring, when everything comes alive, is my season. Psychically there is also a peak. You are really hungry for it. You have everything so perfect, and then the next big wave of growth and flowering comes in! The summer garden has a very, very different splendor to it than the spring garden. It's not so ethereal.

August is a bittersweet month for me; it could be because that was the month my father died. I go through a period in August when things just look dry. The summer is almost over and fall is not quite here. I lose interest, and my garden looks really seedy.

Then in the late fall I always have a tremendous burst of energy when bulb season comes. I need to get the garden back into vital condition. I prune heavily and get everything into a very clean state. It encourages me to know that winter's coming and there will be rebirth. It's interesting that the garden really needs my touch, just like cleaning a house. I like to have my house feel as though everything has been touched when I'm finished cleaning it, and when it has that feeling, it's paradise. Well, it's the same way with the garden.

I plant things way too close, and in the fall, plants that I am no longer in love with, I move to other people's yards. Fall is also a time to rearrange. Some plants definitely belong together, and others don't. Sometimes when you put them in the ground initially, you don't know that; you have to wait a year for the plants to antagonize each other, and then you have to separate them.

Some years I've been less passionately involved, just because my life has been really busy. So much of gardening is systems, like nature. When you don't have your systems together, it takes so much more time to keep things alive. But as I've developed and refined my systems, and the soil and plants have become more healthy, I can develop and tend a larger area in the same amount of time.

I use organic principles because they are the least expensive and the most effective, although I do admit I use snail bait. The soil here in Berkeley is very heavy clay. It can be very rich if it is loosened up,

Mrs. Jackson's backyard. Behind the floral bank on the left is an extensive vegetable garden.

so I've added pounds and pounds of cocoa hulls and rice hulls and mushroom compost, which is shredded hay and horse manure.

I now have a drip watering system which is easy to use, but I also regularly soak the soil by hand where I have shallow-rooted or young plants. I find watering the garden one of the most relaxing things to do. There is something so soothing about watching water spray from the garden hose. It also gives you a regular routine for checking the health of your garden. At least once a month, I try to fertilize by diluting fish emulsion and seaweed, and spraying that on the leaves of my plants.

Gardening is constantly changing, and you have to constantly change with it. What you're working with is nature, this incredible force. And if you work with it, the amount of return is incredible. The more I work with nature, the more I enter an intuitive state of understanding what should go where, and what goes well with each other. It's a process. I go out there at the end of the day and say, "Well, in the morning, I have to water the anchusa, I have to move this over there, and I have to pick all the old rosebuds off." The next day, in the process of doing those three things, the whole day will unfold. I may even discover that I have a snail nightclub that needs annihilation, my terrorist acts!

Gardening takes care, constant nurturing, and staying aware of all the changes the plants go through. You're dealing with these beings, these living things that don't talk or move, but which are very easy to keep alive if you just pay a little bit of attention to them. They don't speak to you in words, but they speak to you intuitively, so that you know what to do for them.

It's an incredibly nurturing and uplifting experience for me to go out and get dirty. I've never looked at gardening as work. For one thing, I enjoy work. I have that ethic. Work to me is not drudgery; that's when you're not repaid for the effort. I work as a general contractor, and even when I'm working full-time, I make time for the garden. And when I come home from a hard day, I go putter for about fifteen minutes in my garden, and walk around and figure out what to do, or do nothing at all.

But my garden definitely reflects how much energy I give to it. I try to have my work schedule as flexible as possible, working in big blocks of time and then taking blocks off. I'm in a position where the skills I have allow me this choice, and I am also very fortunate to have a relatively low overhead.

But, of course, I have great fantasies of having a much greater area. Part of the reason I'm planting the orchard in Eloise's yard is because I just want to see the plants. I've got this vision of the way the earth should look, and that includes flowering fruit trees on her lawn. I don't need to own all this, but it would be great if all of our yards were one large open space over which I had the ultimate say!

My neighbors have called me a "horticultural imperialist," although I wouldn't call myself that. But I am definitely growing gardens wherever I can. And what gives me most pleasure is to meet people who want to garden and to introduce them to this world.

It is one of the nicest things I can do for people. The woman next door and the woman across the street both have nice little gardens, and I taught them. We go to nurseries together and I tell them, "This will do well for you" and so on. They are getting the gist, the feel for it. It's just an absolute passion for me. To have a garden is really a wonderful way to live.

Alice Church with one of her twenty cats.

Alice Church
HARVESTER OF HAPPINESS

Tucked away on a quiet back road outside of Port Orchard, Washington, are the garden and home of Alice and Ed Church. Alice has been a lifelong gardener and it shows; her ornamental garden produces wave after wave of lavish color from spring until fall, and her vegetable garden easily feeds eight people. She has passed her love for plants on to her children and grandchildren, and is doing her best to convert all the neighborhood children as well. For her, gardening not only nourishes and inspires, it has also helped her understand what is truly important in life.

I've gardened all my life. I don't know when my interest in gardening began. I was born this way! I gardened with my father as a child, and with my grandmothers, too. My parents have a picture of me before I was even walking, pulling the heads off the tulips. I had a garden by my playhouse when I was three or four years old. My father planted climbing roses there and I still have the same variety here. It was old Dr. Van Fleet's pink fragrant rose, and it's still one of my most favorite plants.

I have other interests besides gardening—classical music, tole painting, fabric painting—and I love to cook and bake. But gardening is my main interest. I live and breathe it. I dream of flowers, although never in the summertime, just in the winter. My favorite dream is not about my own garden, it's about a garden that I've never seen before. The same things are usually in bloom; there are always delphinium and old-fashioned roses.

My present husband, Ed, and I moved to this lot four years ago. We had sold our other place with just about this many plants on it, and we weren't going to garden anymore. We were tired of it. We're in our late fifties, and we decided that we weren't going to work so hard. So we bought five acres that were just dense woods and gravel; there was no soil here. It was in March of '83 that we came out here and lived in a little truck-back camper while we built this cabin.

But I had some favorite dahlias that I brought, and a few favorite rhododendron and irises. That first spring my husband took a pickax and dug holes in the rocks. We put the dahlia bulbs in and pulled the rocks over them and put water and fertilizer on top, and they just grew! We kept doing a little area here and a little area there and kept on going.

To date, we have planted approximately one acre of flowers plus another half acre of vegetables, and we've put in thirty young fruit trees. And we have berries. I can and freeze almost all of our vegetables because I don't like vegetables and canned goods out of the store. I can about a thousand containers every year, counting jam, fruit, fish, and pickles.

This is where we plan to stay. Ed is a carpenter and was working on a job where they were tearing out some old buildings. We were able to use that salvage to build onto our house, and to build the greenhouse and the shop. My son, his wife, and their five children live in the other house and my mother lives in the trailer, so there are four generations on this property. Ed and I and our son are building

A collection of perennials in Alice's five-acre garden, including several types of irises, peonies, tiger lilies, and phloxes. Her greenhouse is in the background.

without mortgages; we build as we have the money. We plan to let the grandkids work into what we have made here.

Ed was not interested in flowers at first. He was trying to impress me by helping me in the garden, and the first thing he did was to build an arbor. He just got into it, and found out he liked it. He has hauled in pickup loads of barnyard manure, as many as twenty a year. And we bought many, many big dumptruck loads of fir bark, what they call beauty bark, but we till it into the soil rather than use it as a mulch.

I don't garden organically as I use chemical fertilizers. The reason everything is blooming so well is that I go around three or four times a year with buckets of granulated fertilizer, toss it all over, and water it in. I also use insecticides, although I try to ignore the bugs unless there is a very bad problem. The one advantage to this soil is that we don't have moles; it's the first time I've lived in a place where we did not have trouble with them. The ground is so full of rocks that even they can't dig through it.

When my husband comes home from work, we don't sit and talk. We walk the entire property slowly, commenting on the colors and pointing things out to each other. Even if it's raining, we have to go and see what has bloomed during the day. We usually each carry a pair of clippers so we can cut off dead heads or whatever has to be done. If we see a few slugs we take care of them, and if something looks hungry, I'll run and get a cup of fertilizer.

A good part of what I have here I've started from seed and cuttings. When we go to a park, if I see something I like, I get a cutting of it, or I go back and get the seed. When we go to the mountains, I get seeds off the wildflowers. I don't have extremely good luck, but I have better luck than most people, I guess.

My friends always say, "Oh, everything grows for you!" No, everything doesn't grow for me. They only see what grew! A friend will say, "Well, I tried a package of seeds once, and they didn't come up." So? So they didn't come up. So get another package! There are hundreds of dollars worth of special seeds that I send away for that come up and then die, or they don't come up at all. You can't let that discourage you or, at least, I don't let it discourage me.

Something I tell other gardeners that I think is really important: if there are weeds or if something isn't doing well, don't let it bother you. Even if a good plant is dying, cut it off and get rid of it. Don't stress yourself over something that you can't control. If I had to be perfect, if my gardens had to be perfect, with no weeds and no bugs, I'd be nuts! The more relaxed you are about gardening, the more you're going to enjoy it.

I talk to the plants without ever even realizing it. Some time back, I was living next door to this very educated lady. One day I was working in my yard, hoeing away, and I hit a rosebush, scuffing its bark. I said, "Oh, I'm sorry, I didn't mean to hurt you!" My neighbor said, "Who in the world are you talking to?" I hadn't even realized until she said that, that I talk to the flowers all the time. If I have to prune them, I'll tell them, "Now don't be upset, this has to be done," or "I'm not going to hurt you." It's like telling a child to take its medicine or that you have to cut its fingernails. I feel that they know that I'm there. I feel they respond to me.

Every season has a really special meaning. Starting in February, I have the crocus and the reticulata iris, and little alpine bulbs blooming, the bulbs that normally would bloom in the mountains as the snow melts. Then come the daffodils, then the tulips, and about the time the tulips are stopping, the German irises start. Then the Siberian irises come, and the rhododendrons. When the rhododendrons are just finishing up, I have the English irises, the Japanese irises, and the roses starting. As soon as the first blush of roses is done with, then I have gladioluses and dahlias and asters and chrysanthemums in the late fall. By wintertime, because I've worked so hard all summer, canning and freezing all this garden, I'm glad to just sit back and read all my catalogs and books on gardening.

I sit down in the winter to study and research back and forth in my books and in this and that catalog to get the best quality plant. I don't always care about the price. Sometimes price does make a difference, and sometimes it doesn't. By ordering from different companies you learn who is good and who isn't.

Plants are to me like money is to somebody else. The plants are more valuable to me. I used to work for a lady part-time who taught me a lot about plants. But she'd say, "If you had that money in the bank, you could always go get the plant." Well, why in the world would I want money in the bank when I could have the plant?

I do save up, but then I'll do something like put in another greenhouse or go buy a whole bunch of rhododendrons. They're so much better than money. My lands, what good is money? People are so interested in having nice cars and fancy clothes. I have nice

Extending over her lily pond is a Rhododendron fortunei *that Alice has been trying to bonzai for forty years. The deep pink flowers in the center are candelabra primrose and to the right are English pinks, both grown from seed.*

63

clothes and two fake fur coats, but they've been in there on hangers for years. I'm so tired by evening, I don't want to go out.

I feel there's a joy beyond material things. I enjoy what I have because I know that financial gain and material things are not what they're cracked up to be. I've had them. I've had a big, nice new house with a debt. I've had a brand new car with a debt. And I've lost them, and I'm glad they're gone. Those fancy things did not make me happy. They made me stressed because I was afraid they were going to be damaged, or that I was going to lose them.

I don't run up bills, so I don't have to worry about bills. I have a twenty-one-year-old car that's paid for and a little house that's paid for, and I'm happy. I sell a few things from my yard as a sort of favor to my friends, but I don't want to turn my garden into a business. I don't want to be responsible to the public and have to be there all the time. I don't want the money. I want the plants.

If I had unlimited money and could buy everything I ever needed or wanted, where would the joy of getting a bag of tulip bulbs be? Gone, I'm afraid. If I could pay someone to do all my work, the joy of accomplishment would be gone, too. Happiness is all in your mind.

I'm sort of a plant collector. I've worked at nurseries on and off for about thirty-five years in order to buy plants and learn more about them. It's sort of like being a "plantaholic." I think that it probably is an obsession. It's a compulsion, not something that I can even control, or that I would want to control. I see a plant in a nursery and if I have money that I was going to do something else with, I'll buy the plant and let the something else go, like an alcoholic. I sew my own clothes to have extra money for plants.

Fortunately my husband feels the same way I do. I bought him some new work clothes yesterday and he said, "We can't afford that!" Well, I bought a whole bunch of kalmia plants a few days ago worth one hundred dollars, and he felt we could afford that. So he's as bad as I am.

Sometimes I feel like I'm going to explode, I'm so happy. When I picked flowers today and brought them in to smell them, it just made me feel like crying. They're so lovely, so good, and so fleeting. They're going to be gone in another day, but today they're here.

I really love flowers. I don't know how to explain what it is. I love to arrange them, to give them away, and to promote them. When the neighborhood children are going by and they holler, "Hello, Mrs. Church!" I'll say, "Would you like to take some flowers

One section of Alice's neatly tended and highly productive vegetable garden.

to your mother?" and boy, they just flock in here. I never have vandalism, and this is a neighborhood just full of little boys. When they get older, I start giving them bulbs when I cut the bulbs up. I try to remember which kid likes red and which kid likes yellow, and you get them into gardening.

I have two sons and a daughter and all my children like to garden. I never made them help me. I let them be with me in the garden and gave them plants if they wanted them. I let them pick anything they wanted in the garden. I just tried to share the good of it without making them realize that there was work connected. My son who lives here will spend days and days out there sifting out the rocks, as we're still trying to improve the soil.

I have twenty cats. I brought about five cats with me and don't really know where the others come from; I guess people dump them. They just keep coming and find me. When I tame them and can catch them, I take them to the vet to get their shots and have them neutered. If I plant things where I don't want the cats to dig, like crocus bulbs in the fall, I lay fir boughs over them. If they destroy something, I usually don't even notice it because there's so much in this garden.

I've had parakeets for thirty years, and canaries, too. We also had chickens, pigs, and rabbits, but it was just too much, and we recently got rid of them. But I really do love animals. We had orphaned baby skunks come in through the cat door one winter, and I fed them. They would come in and scurry over to the cat food and go back out, or they'd go underneath the stove or rattle around back in the bottom cupboard. The only fighting they did was among themselves. They never sprayed me, but sometimes they would spray each other. It was no big deal. I'd just clean it up with some Clorox.

I want to make my part of the world beautiful and to help people appreciate flowers, and to give to my family. A big reason I have so many different varieties of fruit trees and berries and why we had the chickens, pigs, and rabbits was so that my grandchildren could have that experience, that heritage. About six months ago my ten-year-old granddaughter said, "Grandma, when you get old, can I have some of your things?" And I thought, What in the world? But I said, "Sure. What do you want?" And she said, "Well, I'd like some of your plants and your cats." And I thought, Fantastic! That's success.

What I think I've learned most from gardening is how to be happy. I have an acquaintance who drank a lot and smoked one cigarette after the other; she was always harassing me for spending money on plants. She'd say, "Don't tell me you bought more plants! How in the world can you justify spending so much money on plants when there's so much misery and poverty in this country and in this world?" And one day I answered, "Just because it makes me happy." And she looked stunned and said, "Well, if it would make me happy, I would do it, too. Nothing I have ever done has ever made me happy." Gardening is soul-satisfying. I know so many people that have so much, but they're not happy. I think I'm the happiest person I know.

The Garden as Provider

Linda and Joe Bevilacqua pausing briefly during one of their long and busy summer days.

Linda Bevilacqua
MARKET GARDENER

Linda Bevilacqua and her father, Joe, have created a thriving "You Pick" market garden in Kent, Washington. Market gardens have often been family affairs, but Linda and Joe's collaboration has an unusual component: Joe lost his eyesight over thirty years ago. They are a real team nevertheless, working as hard for each other as they do for their customers, and all the while taking very good care of their rented soil.

My dad got into a fight when he was a little kid and lost one eye. Then, about thirty-five years ago, right after he and my mom got married, he had a detached retina in his good eye and went blind. Farming had been what he had done all of his life, so it kind of messed him up for a lot of years. He really couldn't do much. My mom went to work, and he took care of us kids, getting us off to school and keeping up the house. Nothing ever stopped him.

My mom's a regular old Americanized person, but my dad's folks came from Italy around the turn of the century and settled in Seattle. They were farmers and had a place down in Boeing Field; one of those spots of blacktop used to be their twelve-acre farm. Then the King County Airport moved in, and the county kept condemning more and more of their land until they were forced all the way out.

They bought this little place in Kent, the one acre of ground our house sits on. We rent the five and a half acres next to us, but grow on only five because half an acre is such a swamp. It's clay and right next to the Green River. In the wintertime you can't even walk back there, you'd sink up to your knees!

My sister and brother have never been interested in gardening, but I've been helping my dad garden since I was a child. We always had a garden that was about a third of an acre. My mom would plow it up, and we would pound two stakes in the ground and string wire between them for my dad to follow. I carried the seed can or helped him measure to set the line. Once I was old enough to know what I was doing, I would help him plant, too.

After I got out of high school, I got a regular cashier's job, like anybody has. I hated it. God! Being cooped up all day, watching everything else going on, just drove me crazy! So my dad said, "Well, Linda, we're going to have to do something. We're just sitting here surrounded by grass. Why not grow and sell some corn?" I said, "Why not?"

He always had a tractor, but we went out and bought a little bigger one, and started plowing this mess up. Boy, what a job, since it was just sod. We worked pretty hard that first year to get the ground worked up. I would drive the tractor, and he would walk along behind to make sure it was going all right.

I didn't know anything at all then, and in the beginning we weren't doing it right. I would plow this piece of grown-over sod, but it would only go up on its side and then flop back down again, and the grass would keep right on growing. It wasn't doing any good. So dad would turn it all the way over. A piece of dirt that's about ten inches thick, a foot wide, and several feet long is heavy! But that old geezer got out there and flipped them over. He really worked hard.

That was a terrible mess. It's funny to look back on it now; we can laugh about it. But God, we were tired. We were *really* tired. I think now I'd do it differently. I'd cut a narrower piece; I'm sure it would turn over better. But at the time, I didn't know anything about plowing sod. I'd only plowed dirt that was dirt, where it was natural for it to turn over and break up.

That first year, we did everything wrong. We planted this whole five acres in corn all at the same time, not realizing that we should have staggered it in different patches. We had a lot of overripe corn because it came on all at once and couldn't be picked at once. But people bought it anyway. It was a start, and it taught us a lot.

So we improved every year. After a few years we figured, why don't we see if we can get the ground on the north side of us? We were handling this five acres pretty well, why not get more? So for a few years we had nine acres, and we were doing really well. It was a lot of work, but it also was kind of fun. You feel like you're really getting somewhere.

That land was a lot better piece of ground than this. It was a bit higher and didn't slant back toward the river so much. Wouldn't you know, the owners decided to sell that land and cover it up with a warehouse! One of these days, there'll probably be a warehouse sitting on our place, too. All this land is earmarked for development. That's all there is to it.

Our ground isn't that good. It's not strong enough to support corn, which takes a lot out of the soil. So, after the first couple of years, we started growing other things. We really didn't know what we were doing or what we should plant, but we just kept learning all the time.

This is the ninth year my dad and I have had our garden. That's what we call it: "the garden." Right now, in addition to corn, we have peas and beets, carrots, cucumbers, cabbage, beans, onions, mustard greens, turnips, tomatoes, and garlic. We also grow peppers, celery, potatoes, and fava beans, but they're just for us. An Italian has to have fava beans and a fig tree; our fig tree is over by the house.

Everything except the corn is "You Pick," where people come in and pick their own. My dad and I pick the corn. I drive the truck, of course, and we each have a basket. When the baskets are full, we

Rows of carrots, cabbages, cucumbers, and corn that Linda and Joe weed by hand.

throw the ears onto the bed of the pickup. Of course, the corn is harder for him to find, but he does just fine. He knows when the corn is ripe, better than I do. I don't know how he does it, but he can tell a good ear just by the feel. We sell the cornstalks to some people who have cows. What they don't buy, I disk back into the ground. You've got to put something back in.

Fortunately, we don't have to water a lot. We sprinkle a few things, but we never put any water on the corn. The water table here is pretty high, being right next to the river. We find if we cultivate a lot, cutting off the little side roots, the main root gets stronger and goes down deeper. We do this with a cultivating tractor, but we also do a lot of the weeding by hand. With this wet ground we have a lot of horsetail and some quack grass, all things that have long roots. If we don't pull them out, they will take over. The morning glories are terrible, too. So, while we have our garden, we beat the weeds back every year.

I do all the plowing and planting, but we do the weeding together. Dad's real good at it. We have a hand cultivator, and I go down the sides of the rows and knock out the weeds there, so we only have the strip where the plants actually are to weed. We get down on our hands and knees and go down the rows together. Of course, I get to the end of my row first, so I come back and help him. But it is surprising how much work he gets done. For example, carrots are harder than a lot of things to weed, and he really gets many of the weeds out. We weed three rows at a time, rows that are 250 feet long. It takes me about three hours to get down to the end of my rows. After he has come to the end of his, it only takes me about an hour and a half to go back over them and finish what he has done.

That's a time when we visit a lot. He tells me stories about the old days, when his folks had a farm and he was a kid. I hear the same stories every year, but he tells them like they just came into his mind fresh. He doesn't change his stories each year, he just sticks to the facts. Some of his favorite stories are about Liar Number One and Liar Number Two. They were guys who would just make stories up, the bigger the better.

Our plants are pretty healthy, so we don't have to use too much insecticide. We do have to spray for cabbage bugs and, occasionally, for aphids on the beans. But other than that, we've never had any real problem. We're not organic farmers, but we try to stay away from chemicals as much as we can because we don't like them either. It's bad enough living next to a noisy highway and sucking in all the exhaust from the traffic that goes by day and night. Boeing is right down the road, and they're open twenty-four hours. At Christmas they close for about ten days; everyone gets that time off, and it's a real break for us as well.

We don't put in cover crops during the winter. It takes a while to pick all the corn and the late cabbage. By the time we are finished harvesting in the fall, there isn't enough time to plant anything; it's just too wet to work the fields.

We can't do much in March, so our season starts in April, and it's over by the end of October. By then I'm tired out and sick of the whole thing. We take one nice rest—until the following April. My dad takes the winter off in a serious way. He sits in his chair and sleeps most of the day. Then he complains about all his aches and pains, which is all right, too. I guess he deserves to. He's seventy-one years old now—getting up there a little—and it's time for him to slow down.

I really like having the winter off too because the summer is just work, work, work. Even when it rains the ground doesn't get too wet, and we go out and work anyway. When you see everyone going to the beach and you're working in the hot sun, it sometimes gets to you. We start at about seven in the morning and sometimes the days don't end until about nine o'clock at night. I've even had to turn on the car headlights so I could read the scale to see what customers have, they pick so late.

My dad has always been a bug about having a clean garden. He would never grow anything he couldn't take care of. That's the way he taught me, and that's good enough for me, too. What you plant, you have to be there to take care of. You have to be ready to stay there every day, if that is what it takes. Even if you want to go have fun, you can't do it.

He really tries to take good care of this soil, even though we're only renting it. I'll tell you a funny story about that. Long Acres Racetrack is nearby. They keep the horses real clean so there's not a lot of manure; it's mostly straw. Usually they truck it to a mushroom farm down in Oregon, but that company went bankrupt, and the straw and manure started piling up. A fellow I know told me about it and contacted them. They brought us a load in a forty-foot trailer, ten feet deep and I don't know how wide. They pushed this pile out and it was all chopped up! It was horrible. They'd run it through a grinder and you couldn't get a pitch fork into it to spread. But because my dad thought it would be good for the soil, he came up with a scheme to spread it all out on the ground this spring.

We laid down a piece of plywood and hooked a chain and tractor to it and loaded the straw on. It was horrible to try to spread because you had to kind of push it off with the pitchfork. So then we hooked up a broken-down loader on one of the tractors, and just pushed the manure onto this piece of plywood. Then I drove the tractor into the fields and spread it out with a shovel; it was a lot of trips and a lot of work.

Now, some people would think we were crazy to do it—they really would—because all most people do year after year is go over to a fertilizer salesman, buy all this granulated fertilizer, and put it on the ground. We have to use that kind of fertilizer, too, but my dad likes to do things the hard way sometimes, and he's worried about our piece of ground getting too weak.

We may work hard, but we're always happy, we always make money, and we don't have any debts. God, who wants to go into debt for something like gardening, when you never know how it's going to turn out? So far, we've never gotten messed up in any way, but we could. There's never been a late frost that really wrecked things or bugs that ate everything up, and no one came in and built a warehouse while we had something growing; that happened after the season ended.

We never know if we can rent this ground from one year to the next. The fellow who owns it could sell it any time. When that happens I think it would be the end of our garden because my dad is very cautious. He wants to live next door to where he works, like we do here. He doesn't like the idea of having to load up equipment and take it to a different place.

Our customers have been coming for years. They just love it. It's convenient for people from Seattle, Auburn, Federal Way, Maple Valley—everywhere. If we moved out to other land, I don't know who would find us. If we moved out to where the land is good, then there would already be competition. If we moved out to where the ground is bad, what's the use of that? It's been ideal here for us as long as it lasts. When it's over, I guess it'll just be over. That'll be that.

But I don't know what I'll do then. I don't like working for other people. I like being independent and working for myself. You work harder, but it's different. It's much nicer. We can make money

Zucchini and onions are in the foreground, and bush and pole beans are on the right. In the distance, Joe stakes tomato plants; on the far right is the warehouse built on the five acres they used to farm.

because we keep our overhead low. If you want to spend a lot of money, you can buy one nice tractor that has all these modern three-point attachments, but we like to keep our costs down. It saves us from going into debt.

We get all these ancient, broken-down tractors where something has to hook up in a different way on each one. Over the years we've bought five tractors; the oldest one is a '39; the next one is a '41. We've got two '48s. The newest one is a '52, and it's the biggest piece of junk! Our machinery may be old but it works, or most of the time it works, because we take good care of it. We fix them all the time, again and again. I do some of the repair work, and I'm good about maintenance; that's another thing Dad's always taught.

I plant the peas, beets, carrots, cucumbers, and even the cabbage with a heavy old hand planter. We planted the beans by hand this year because the machine doesn't work well on that type of seed. We did what we did in the old days: I strung a line, and Dad planted them behind. The tomatoes we start from seed in the house in February, and when they get about an inch high, we plant them out in the hot bed, which has a heat cable in the ground. I have some rabbits, so we work the rabbit manure into that soil. By the time May comes along, the frosts are over and the seedlings are big enough to plant outside.

The sports stuff that people do to keep fit is nonsense to me. I can't see sitting down at a desk all day and then running around after work to keep fit, when you can have one job that combines the whole thing that you can make money at. Well, like I say, it's good for me. I'm sure it wouldn't work for a lot of people.

My boyfriend isn't interested in gardening at all. He's interested in machinery, and he's been fixing everything around the place. It's been a real help, but I don't think he's too interested in actually farming. You've got to get down on your hands and knees, and there is a lot of slow, boring work, just hard, sweating, dirty stuff. I don't think he's really cut out for that.

But I find it satisfying. You've got to care about what you're doing. And it's nice to know that what you're working so hard on is something people can eat, instead of some silly plastic thing. To tell you the truth, I enjoy every step of it, from the time you start out till you're finished.

The first thing you do is go out, hook up your disk, and drive around disking in the winter weeds, even though it's wet. The ground looks nice and brown and all fluffed up. Then you get in and start plowing it. It looks beautiful when it's plowed. Even though plowing is a lot of hard work, you enjoy it. Then you disk it up to get ready for planting, and that looks good. Then you plant it and can see the nice tire marks if you've done it by machine, or the footprints, if you pushed the hand planter. You say, "Boy, that looks nice."

Then when the seeds first come up, that looks nice. And then they get up a little bigger, and hey, that looks nice. And then the weeds start, so you start pulling the weeds. Once you've gone through and weeded a patch, boy, you know, that looks nice. And on and on. And then, once it's picked, it doesn't look so great anymore, but you have the satisfaction of knowing that it grew and you sold everything. And then you turn under as much as you can, and you're back to nice brown dirt again, and boy, that looks nice.

It makes me feel good to be growing food. I enjoy being strong and healthy, able to work and sweat and get dirty. For some reason I like that. There's a lot of variety in what you do, with the tractors and the handwork. And it takes endurance, too. You feel good when you find out that you can stay out there for hours and hours and hours and not give up. I guess you get used to it. When I was a kid I used to really melt when the weather got hot; I couldn't move. Now I can do anything.

My mom is totally uninterested in the garden, and that's okay, too. She has a regular nine to five job, and she works plenty hard. My folks don't socialize a lot. They don't care about all that stuff, but by selling vegetables, we meet a lot of nice people. Many of them are guys of my dad's generation, and he really has a ball. They're just happy to talk about when Boeing was just starting out, and remembering this place or that. It's helped him a lot that way. It really sparks his interest.

It's nice to give people an honest deal, to treat people fairly, and be treated fairly. About 90 percent of the people who come here are just as honest as you could ever want anybody to be, but there are those that cheat. Some people eat as much as they possibly can as they pick, and even stuff things into their purses. Maybe they've had a hard life, and that's the only way they can survive, but it makes me really mad.

With gardening you sure learn the value of hard work. If you don't keep at it, you don't end up with anything. But we have a lot of fun growing things. It's satisfying, from start to finish. It's interesting. It's varied. It's a challenge. You get to meet a lot of nice people. You learn a lot, about human nature too. It's just a good life.

Charles Bushman and his compost bins which double as containers for growing squash.

Charles Bushman
MAXIMUM PRODUCER

Anyone going by Charles and Marie Bushman's home in Portland, Oregon, would know they were expert gardeners by the profusion of vegetables and roses that fills their front yard. They are constantly trying new ways to grow more food on their one-sixteenth acre urban lot. Charles has even grafted one apple tree with ten different varieties. They grow ornamentals and exotics as well, but most of all, the Bushmans love the pleasure and challenge of feeding themselves almost exclusively from their own garden.

When I was about six years old, I used to get my fanny pushed out to the garden. Then it was not voluntary. Prior to the time I was twelve, I didn't think much of gardening. I liked to eat, but I didn't think much of producing it. However, by the time I was fourteen, I was growing a garden in the summertime professionally. We had a farm and I grew beans as one way of making spending money.

My grandparents had an orchard in Scappose, Oregon, that had been planted in the 1880s. When they had a tree that wasn't altogether what they wanted and a new variety would come along, my grandfather would graft on the new variety. I used to watch. As soon as I got a little older and we had trees, I started doing the grafting. I still enjoy it. Sometimes you get 75 percent, sometimes you get 10 percent.

In our garden we were able to save a little of the stock from my grandfather's orchard: we have some of the Lady apple and the Kings. We also have a Perle d'Or rose from one that my grandmother planted in the 1880s. She died in 1899, but we have carried that rose through, so it is probably one hundred years old.

My wife, Marie, and I garden together. We probably spend about two hours every day in the garden if we're here. It's all on an automated watering system so we can travel when we want. Marie raises all her own bedding plants. This year, I think every one of them grew because we furnished a lot of tomato plants and different exotic plants, like orchids, to sell at the Master Gardeners' plant sale in the spring.

We moved into this home March 12, 1940, and we've gardened all of those years. Even when I was away in the service, from '42 to '45, Marie maintained the garden. For many years we had a lawn in the front and backyard, and grew vegetables in the back of our lot. About eight years ago, we had to decide whether to put in a new lawn out front, as our lawn had red thread and every disease that came along. I said, "To heck with it! I never did like grass anyhow; we'll garden the full length." We like our food, and we like it fresh.

We built our greenhouse in 1954. We had taken out life insurance policies on our two daughters for twenty-pay life so that at twenty years old, they would have paid-up policies. But then, when our youngest was five, she came down with acute lymphocytic leukemia. Even at her age, she loved flowers, so after she was gone, we decided to use some of the money on a greenhouse that would be a memorial to her. Our other daughter wasn't into gardening too much when she was real young, but she is now. She has two-and-

The Bushmans' front yard is filled with peas in the spring, followed by corn in the summer and fall.

one-half acres in Corvalis and farms part of it, growing onions and melons and all of those things.

I started keeping bees in 1928 when I was in high school. I like to work with them. Marie was very allergic to them and took shots. Now, if they sting her, they don't bother her much. There aren't too many bees in the neighborhood, so it makes a real difference to our garden, with the apples especially. When the bee inspector was here a while back, he said there aren't too many other hives right close.

We have a neighbor who has two apple trees, a June Red and a Gravenstein. The Gravenstein is not self-fertile. It has to have a pollenizer. A few years ago he was complaining to me that he wasn't getting any apples. Although the tree was over thirty years old, I cut some flower branches from my Lodi and Golden Delicious, put them in a can of water, and hung them in his tree. Every time I'd do that, he'd have over forty pounds of apples because the bees would move over to his trees.

I take very good care of our ground, but I don't garden organically. We use commercial, or chemical, fertilizers, and we use sprays because I don't like worms, either in my apples or my cabbage. But we try to hold spraying to a minimum. We brought in eleven cubic yards of horse manure this winter for additive to the ground, and it helps. In the winter, just as soon as the corn in the front and backyard is out, we put in winter rye. When it is about two feet high, we chop it back in with a tiller. The cornstalks and pea vines all go back into the ground, too.

We compost as well and produce so much of it that we give it away to three different neighbors across the street. This is even after I double-spade an area, take the bottom part out to mix with next year's compost, and add compost to the top part.

A few of our neighbors have gotten involved in gardening and have started their own compost piles, too. It really used to irk me to see people giving their grass clippings to the garbage man instead of working them back into the soil where they would do some good.

We used to put our apple tree prunings into the compost pile the way they were, but two years ago we got a chipper and that really makes a difference. It used to be that some of those fairly good-sized limbs wouldn't be rotted down after four years, but now we put them through the chipper, and they go right to work.

We make our own potting soil which consists of one bucket of peat moss, one bucket of vermiculite, one bucket of perlite, one bucket of sand, and a half-bucket of sterilized compost. We make up two yards of it at a time, and it's always worked very well. In fact, when we plant our peas in the spring, we put the seed on the ground and use this potting soil to cover it. Rather than having the peas surrounded by cold clay that holds a lot of water, you have a well-drained media for it to come up through.

Our Oregon giant beans grow twenty feet high, and we have to harvest them with a ladder. Lily Miller Co. quit producing them, but Ed Hume, the garden editor of the *Seattle Times*, has them. We like them much better than Blue Lakes or Kentucky Wonders or any of the rest; these have some meat to them. Because they grow twice as high, you get double the production on the same amount of ground. To get maximum production in the space we have, we buy the pelletized carrot and lettuce seed and plant them with tweezers in order to place them the proper distance apart.

We've probably tried every tomato from Bonny Best on to Beefsteak and all of Burpee's different varieties, but now we just

Beans, lettuce, and carrots grow in the backyard. Charles plants the carrot seed with tweezers so that he can get maximum production from this small plot.

grow Park's Greenhouse tomatoes. They produce for us in the greenhouse through December. Then, because tomatoes are a perennial, we take cuttings, winter them over in the greenhouse, and plant them in the spring. They will produce about twice as fast as those from seed because they already have the flower tips on them, so we really get the most out of our tomatoes.

We plant our potatoes under the apple trees in February, so they get most of their growing done before the apple trees leaf out. By June they're getting pretty leggy, but we don't expect mature potatoes; we grow them for the small potatoes, which we like.

We can all our own food, even cherries and peaches and pears. We go up to Hood River or the Dalles to get those and bring them home in order to can them our own way. We buy very little canned food, maybe canned pineapple for a salad once in a while. We even grew pineapple once in the greenhouse. All you have to do is take a pineapple top, put it in sand, root it, and then put it in soil. It requires warm temperatures and lots of light. The first year we had one pineapple, and then the plant stooled out and had two pineapples on it the next year. People in the islands say, "You can't do that!"

The part of the gardening process I enjoy the most is eating it. I like fresh food—food that's tasty—and it's challenging to see what you can and can't grow. People come along and ask the question, "How do you do it?" So we give them the grand tour, including our food drying in the basement and our freezer. If we can get one out of ten, or even twenty, to start growing their own food and find out what good food tastes like, then I figure we've accomplished something.

Charles gets a great crop of beans by growing them on a twenty-foot-high trellis.

Debbie Carlson in her herb and everlasting garden.

Debbie Carlson
ALASKAN GARDENER

At a time when many of their contemporaries have settled into a high-tech world, Debbie Carlson and her husband, Jim, have pursued an alternate route. They have created a productive food and everlasting garden in circumstances that would discourage most of us: a cool mountain summer, topsoil only two or three inches deep, and no running water. Through sacrifice, a lot of hard work, and careful attention to detail, they have created their own unique version of "living lightly off the land" outside of Cooper Landing, Alaska.

The biggest animal pests in our garden are moose. Our sled dogs do keep the moose at bay somewhat, but we have had the moose charge the dogs and run through the garden. Oftentimes they will eat a lot of the cabbages, and there goes your crop right there. They also eat the little raspberry shoots, so my raspberry vines keep getting pruned. We do have coyotes and bear in the area, but they have not come close. Fortunately, the snowshoe hare haven't discovered our garden yet because we don't want to fence it in.

Jim and I have been together for ten years and gardening for almost that long, but in different places. He's done a lot of the harder labor, but we are equally involved. We both have our different fancies, but they are very complementary. He is more interested in doing what Alaska is best at doing, root crops. Our winter fare is rutabagas, turnips, carrots, parsnips, and potatoes; they store very well here, too. I like herb gardening. Although it is very difficult here, it's still satisfying to me. And I like playing with everlasting flowers, and growing some of the greens. So I'm on the top, and he's hunting in the ground.

When we first moved to Cooper Landing from Anchorage, we dug an eight-by-ten-foot root cellar. It's eight feet down into the ground, and then we blocked it up, making a little underground house. Sometimes in root cellars water will collect in the bottom, or it's too humid or too warm, or the vegetables freeze. We were lucky that the moisture and coolness of ours turned out to be the perfect combination for storing food, and that all the work we did turned out to be worth it. In addition to the food we can, freeze, or dry, I store potted herbs and other perennials over the winter in the cellar, too.

We built a greenhouse on top of the root cellar, and use half of it to grow things and the other half as a little guest house where people can stay when they come. It's a nice place in the spring when the sun starts to come up, a real warm spot. We lived there while we were building our workshop, and it was fun in the winter. We watched the snow and could hear the rain. It's almost like being in a tent; you get to hear everything. When we moved into the workshop—where we are living now while we build our house—we couldn't hear the owls at night and the coyotes, and all of a sudden we felt like we were really shutting ourselves in.

We don't have electricity. Instead we have two generators for power tools and lights during the winter, and a solar panel which generates enough energy for our TV, tape deck, and radio. We don't have a well; we collect rainwater from the gutters and store it in a big seven-hundred-gallon tank. We do get enough rain, hundreds of gallons at a time, and that lasts weeks. Our nine sled dogs actually take more water than the garden, and even in the winter they are fed a large quantity of water to keep them from dehydrating.

When we need more water, I have a four-wheel-drive Suzuki and a little trailer which we load up with buckets and take down to the creek. We can haul probably eighty or ninety gallons at a time that way. That's not enough for a deep watering, but once you get the plants germinated, the roots go down real fast. I have already installed a drip irrigation system in the beds, but it was so rainy this summer, we didn't need to use it.

We've had to learn how to cope with the ups and downs here, but we've been pretty happy that it has worked out because we made a lot of sacrifices. We melt snow in the winter; that gives us enough water, as we don't have any gardening needs then, of course. We have some alternative systems planned: to put a cistern in the house and use an old-fashioned hand pump. We have a sauna out in the woods, a bathhouse-type thing for when we want to take more than sponge baths.

It's not easy; but it's prohibitive to live the way we want to live and have a well. Wells here have to go very, very deep—at least four-hundred feet—and you have to have a huge generating system to pump it. If we do that, we've defeated all the purposes we had for coming here in the first place: to live in the quiet of nature and to try to not be so dependent on town to earn money. This is a recreation and retirement area, and there aren't many jobs.

There may come a time when we will be physically incapacitated and not able to lift the jugs of water we do now, and then we might have to have a well. But right now, we're healthy enough to do it. We know that's a real blessing; it's not a burden but a challenge, and it's fun to see it work.

Jim has not had a regular job for the last two years as he's been working full-time doing all the building. I help on that when I can; I've peeled a lot of logs! I've been commuting to Anchorage for three years now, where I have a house, garden, and greenhouse, because I work there three days a week as a dental hygienist. I've been a hygienist for fifteen years, so I have a real solid practice, and don't want to leave it right now. It is taking our maximum to keep two houses and two cars and everything going on this part-time work; it's very challenging. But as soon as we get our house done and our expenses down, we'll probably be just fine.

Debbie and Jim's garden in front of the combined root cellar-guest house they built.

It's about a two-hour drive from here to Anchorage in good weather, and quite a contrast, going from no water and dirty hands to a city environment that's totally sterile, and getting more sterile every day. My house in Anchorage has an unobstructed southern exposure and running water, so the garden can be managed more conveniently. But I put less and less time into my garden there every year; I'm weaning myself away.

I grow a lot of flowers there and dry them and bring them down here to make arrangements. I'm trying to learn how to grow the same flowers here, before I give my other home up. I'm just interested in it. I will always want to keep growing and to have flowers around. I make special flower arrangements for people, but it's a labor of love; I don't like selling them because then I feel I have to see a profit, and I can't really get my money back.

In Anchorage, I find that by the time I gather materials, go shopping, go to work, keep up my house, and all the other necessary kind of things, I don't have time to relax. But here, I can browse around; I have time to pick things, and time to wander here and there. I don't think gardening is fun unless you have that kind of time. To us, time is the real luxury, not money. I respect my free time. It makes it all worthwhile.

My husband found this place when cross-country skiing on a trail the gold miners used going from Hope via Cooper Landing to Seward, a seaport. It is bounded and protected on two sides by state and federal land. The homesteaders had decided to subdivide; they were older and their children weren't interested in living here, as often happens when children were raised one way and want to live another way.

That's what happened to me. I was raised in Indianapolis, Indiana, and often wonder how I came to choose this. My sister and brother have life-styles that are exactly the opposite of mine. Maybe I can do this because I've had the other, and I still have it when I go to Anchorage. I've never lived here 100 percent of the time, but I'd like to try it.

I don't really know how I got involved in gardening. My folks always gardened, but to me, it was unpleasant work. It was often-times very hot and humid and buggy in Indiana. It was more chore work. For some reason I'm not as bothered by the bugs up here, and I really like cool temperatures to work outside. I was from the generation where, in the sixties and seventies, people were doing earth things instead of high-tech things, and so I just surrounded myself with people who were doing what seemed a natural thing to do. I found out it worked, that there was a lot of satisfaction to it.

But I think that if I wasn't in Alaska and had to garden year round, I would probably burn out. I prefer to be only actively doing it for three or four months, then thinking and planning for a few months, and then starting seeds indoors—that kind of thing. It's a constant change that way.

I never quite tire of the harvesting, of having to tend to the plant itself. I like the cycle that we have up here, even though it is very challenging. We have a long summer gardening season because of the almost continual daylight. That's why you hear about the big vegetables in Alaska. They do need a lot of water and fertilizer because of the intensive growing season.

As we have been building, we have scraped every piece of soil off the ground and built up all our raised beds with that. We really appreciate our soil because we don't have a lot of it. The topsoil was only two or three inches thick, but it was virgin forest. It was pretty organic and nutritive for the first few years, and we didn't add any fertilizer because we really didn't need it. Now we can see that we are going to have to start doing that.

We don't compost on a large scale. I've done it on a small scale in a little barrel because I don't like throwing anything away. I plan on doing more later, after we've finished building. You have to have a pretty good sun site for it. Our neighbor does; he also has electricity and a generating system, where he can really grind the compost up well. You've got to get the pieces really small, as it still takes a couple of years for things to break down. But we plan to be here a long time, and those years do fly by.

The natural ground cover here is so fragile that we brought in all of our logs for firewood and for our buildings over the snow during the winter; if you do any firewood gathering or disturbing of natural vegetation, this land doesn't regenerate. We have put gravel on all of the paths on our property so that people will stay on them and not haphazardly walk around. We don't even walk through the woods here, unless it's to pick berries, because the plants we crush don't grow back again. Even the game tend to follow their own paths.

We love winter. I've had my share of going to Hawaii in the winter, and I've traveled around the world a bit. Maybe that's why I'm more satisfied to stay home. I still plan trips, but our cycle is such that when we're done with gardening and harvesting in October, we're tired.

Usually in November and December, I make the things for Christmas. In January, the sun is coming back our way, and we start watching how it creeps up above the mountains. We chose to live on the south side of these mountains so we could have sun all winter long; we're the only people in Cooper Landing who have that. Even though we live in Alaska and it's dark in the winter, we're still sun-oriented; when we see it, it gives us a real direct boost. I think I probably appreciate it more living here than if I lived elsewhere.

In January, we really have a good time going through the seed catalogs and planning, so winter doesn't seem too long; it might even be our favorite time. We gear ourselves to winter camping, skiing, and running the dogs. We do a lot of astronomy and indoor projects, and read a lot, and putter.

We can hardly wait for snow, not only to do the things we like, but because it's quite dark in the winter without the snow. It's really a light source because of its reflectivity. When you live in the woods without electricity, and you're dependent on your eyes adjusting to whatever available light there is, you learn to really appreciate it. It gets dark by four or five in the afternoon during the winter, and that doesn't give us enough time to do all the outdoor things we have to do, like haul wood or burn slash. With a real heavy snow cover, we have worked outdoors by the moonlight until late at night.

I get the biggest kick from the rain. My patients complain, "Oh, the rain!" But I feel like a farmer, and really appreciate it. We don't get downpours here, like in other parts of the country. It drips a lot, but you can still go out and play, or go fishing or hiking. It's not the kind of rainfall where you get immediately soaked. Here, because of the cold, you can't let yourself get soaked! When it's raining hard, I'm out there bucketing; it's like playing in the rain. When I was a kid, I always wanted to do that. I think it's fun and, of course, I can always come in and get warm.

My husband and I like to feel more a part of the natural cycles. We only differ in that he would use more hazardous materials to control pests and fungi than I am comfortable with. Here we let the gardening cycle happen more naturally than if we were in Anchorage. We mainly garden for the health of it, not to save money or because we need the food. If we add our labor to our gardening costs, it would be cheaper to buy our food at the market.

I can't get excited about taking care of a house. I really have a craving to be outside, and definitely choose to be outdoors more than indoors. I want to be a part of anything that is alive and changing, and like everything there is to do about a garden. I'm ready in the spring to plant, I'm ready to see it come up, I'm ready to start eating, and I'm ready to start harvesting. Every aspect is intriguing and different.

Gardening has a spiritual aspect, too; there's that kind of satisfaction as well. It's just a work of art. I'm not an artist in the sense that I can sit down and paint something, but to me, watching it happen the way it is supposed to is like witnessing the evolution of a work of art. It is not, of course, created by my own hand. I'm just there tending it. I like going out there and touching everything. I like being in the garden and seeing it all.

Lho Kazarian harvesting some berries in her backyard.

Lho Kazarian
FRUIT TREE LOVER

Lho, who moved from Sweden to the United States many years ago, was surprised to discover in mid-life that she loved gardening. Because of her concern about pesticides in food and soil, she decided to try to feed herself and her husband almost entirely from their organic garden in Sacramento, California. The experiment was a success, and, in the process, she developed an interest in edible landscaping and a passion for fruit trees.

I have fifty fruit trees on my quarter-acre lot. I hunted down the
smallest dwarf trees I could get. I have a pineapple guava, a lemon
guava, a strawberry guava, four kumquats, a dwarf fig tree, Santa
Rosa and Satsuma plums, Fuyu persimmons, and semidwarf black,
Tartarian, and Bing cherry trees. I also have a pomegranate,
carambola, two apple trees, and a plumcot (which is a cross between
a plum and apricot), a tangelo, a Mars grapefruit, a Valencia orange,
a Washington Navel, a Meyer lemon, and a lime tree. Then there is a
jujube, almond trees, apricots, loquats, a pineapple quince, a little
carob tree, and a Babak papaya. I also have a tree tomato, a tree that
grows up about eight to twelve feet, with a purplish red tomato.

Of course I have a jaboticaba, a raisin tree, and a papaw. I have
another interesting tree called the golden arengela. It is a very pretty
tree that you can enjoy looking at, but it has teeth on the upperside
of the leaf and isn't meant to be touched. I also grow boysenberries,
raspberries, kiwis, grapes, passion fruit, kiwano, and pepino dulch.

I have mainly taught myself and learned from books. I like that
because I can go at my own speed. I also became a member of the
California Rare Fruit Growers. I thought that we should have a
Sacramento chapter so we could learn more from one another. So I
invited the president and his wife to come for a meeting with the
other members in this area. He and his wife stayed overnight, and
when he left he said, "You now have a Sacramento Valley chapter." I
said, "We do?" because we had not yet picked a president and
chairman. "Yes," he said, "I baptise you."

My mother is in her eighties and lives in the country in the
northern part of Sweden. She is a tremendous gardener, and was
never afraid to take a shovel and dig. But I had never gardened until
my husband and I moved to a home in east Sacramento. It had a
small garden with hardpan soil. The first year I planted carrots, and
when I tried to pull them up, I got only the green part. The rest were
stuck in the ground and we had to use a shovel to pry them out. I
was very disappointed. Eventually, I had thirty-nine different
vegetables growing there in a nine-by-thirteen-foot plot.

But I was afraid to put in trees, so I said to my husband, "Let's
move somewhere where we can really grow a lot of things." I am
very afraid of the poisons which are sprayed on food. You read so
much about cancer, and I don't think it's good for the earth, either.
So I said, "Couldn't we have our own garden and our own fruit
trees, so I can handle it my way and know there is no poison on it?"
He said, "Okay."

We moved here to find out what working in the best farmland was like. I wanted a bigger garden. We ended up with a bigger house. I think it should have been a smaller house and bigger garden! But we chose the corner lot so our house could be in the middle, surrounded by a circle of trees.

Unfortunately, after we bought the house we discovered that the builders had dumped a lot of gravel and building leftovers because it was the corner lot, and then just covered it all up. It was very sad. I cried many, many times over it because it took so much of my time and money to remove that, and it was such hard work. But I didn't give up until I had dug everything out.

Since there is so much clay in the soil, Mr. Moorhead—head of the University of California at Davis's Extension—told me to replace the dirt and put in an underground drainage system so that nothing would stay soggy. He also said to build up little hills for the trees. As you can see in my yard, the trees are on mounds so they don't get

Lho's fruit-tree-filled front yard.

too wet. Both suggestions were good things because I have never had a tree die from root rot.

I never spray any poison. I have been battling aphids; I found out that when you grind lemon peel in the Osterizer with garlic and hot pepper, drain it through a nylon stocking, and spray it on roses, the aphids don't like it. I also tip-prune my trees because the aphids usually like the tip of the branch. To get rid of the ants that carry the aphids, I mix regular flour with borax, half of each. I spread it out on the cement, so I won't poison the ground. In three days, the floor is black with dead ants because they get diarrhea and kind of weaken to death.

I call my mother in Sweden quite often. After the nuclear accident at Chernobyl, she told me how they had to bury the reindeer's meat because of the radioactivity. They had to import food from Israel, and were afraid to drink the milk or to grow things in the garden and eat them. They tried to get soil that was not contaminated from underneath buildings for gardening. Everything is still being tested. Can you believe it?

My husband and I are Bible students, and the Bible says that God is going to destroy those who destroy the earth. It talks about how people have ruined the earth. Believe me, this is a prophecy. I feel it will come true, that it is going to get worse. I have a garden not only because I enjoy it, but also to prove to myself and others that it is possible to garden without poisoning things. Even if I prove it only to myself, I get a certain satisfaction out of it.

I do believe in Bible prophecies, and I think it's sad that the human race has been so insensitive to one another by making wars and poisoning the earth with chemicals and radiation, and by turning away from good. But how can you fight the whole world alone? How could I? I can only do my little part, the best way I know how. I am trying to do what I think is right in my heart.

If I had more land I'd have cows and horses. But I'm in my middle fifties, and there's a time when you draw the line and say, "This is it. Don't go any further." We do have a cat, and I feed the birds. There is also a lot of work in the garden that still has to be done, but everything takes time, so I move along with time.

The birds are my little helpers. I feed them all the leftover cat food, oatmeal, and bread crumbs. I even give them health food, like the leftover flax seed and sesame seed I use in my breads. And I provide water for them. If there is no food out there, they come and peck at my window, like they're saying, "You're late with breakfast!"

I figured out I must be spending an average of six hours a day in the garden. We have calculated with all the landscaping we have done, and having to dig out all the builder's junk, and changing our minds on some things, that the garden has cost us thirty thousand dollars. I work in the garden during the day, and in the evening I work as an interior designer. It works pretty well that way because people prefer evening appointments so they can talk with their husbands or wives and families. All the money I make has gone into the garden. We haven't figured out how much money we have saved with the garden, but we do eat from it all year around, as we are mostly vegetarian. In Sacramento, you can grow vegetables in the fall and winter, too.

My husband mows the lawn. He's not much for planting and harvesting, but as the trees have grown and the garden has developed into a better-looking place, he's taken more pleasure in it.

I think the biggest challenge with gardening is after you plant something, you have to nurse it like a little baby until it reaches the first few inches above the ground. The biggest thrill is to watch it grow.

I think it is something built-in in human beings: the minute we are born, we feel we want to be in touch with nature. We are part of nature. I think God created all those beautiful trees for us to enjoy and to be in touch with. It's a relationship. You just don't give up a good relationship. It's like a marriage; you have to work on it. My garden is part of my marriage, too. I only have one son and one grandson from a previous marriage, and I don't see them very often, so my little trees are my family, too. I really love them.

It sounds silly, but sometimes I just grab a branch and hug it. My trees give me so much pleasure, even though they wear me out. But doesn't a family do the same thing? And remember, all of the trees, shrubs, vegetables, and you name it out there—they never hurt your feelings, do they? People do. Plants don't. I draw an energy out of my garden to survive and heal my wounds that have come maybe from being hurt in other areas in life. The energy I get from the garden is an ointment on those sores. I need it, and I'm so happy it's there.

You're so protected in a garden because you know there's nothing that is going to hurt you. It's just open; all the trees' arms are open. The garden seems to say, "Come. Here is love. Here is enjoyment. Soak it all up. Be my sponge."

We have a saying in Sweden, "You're not able to love until you've been loved," and I think that goes with the garden, too. If the garden has always been loved, it shows. I think that plants and trees

Many of Lho's dwarf fruit trees are in pots so they can be moved into the gazebo on the left during the winter.

have feelings. Don't they give us a message when they look sick? Look at my neighbor's tree. It is neglected and sick. It is screaming for help. It hurts me to see it, and it hurts that I can't go out there and make it happy. I even feel that it suffers not only from malnutrition but also from jealousy, when it senses the care my trees get.

Gardening is a lot of work and people who don't have time to garden and keep the garden neat and clean should not start it. It's not fair to neighbors to have a messy yard. It's not fair to the family, or to themselves. It's like raising children, you have to take care of them. And you have to feel proud of everything. When you leave the garden at night, you have to know that you did your best to take care of it.

As many trees as I have, I put only trimmings in the street the night before pick-up for the garbage man, at most only two or three times a year, when I do heavy pruning. I always put the grass clippings in the compost pile. It upsets me terribly that people use the street as a dumping place. To me that's the floor of the neighborhood, and we're all roommates on this floor.

It's as if you and I were roommates and you put a potato peel on the floor and left it there for a week. How could I enjoy living there? I hope someday there is a law so that people cannot dump things on the street, especially here in Sacramento, because it's so hot and it's so unhealthy to have refuse lie there. Cars run over it, and children run over it with their bicycles and play in it.

My dream is to be an edible landscaping consultant, to help people develop their yards into beautiful little paradises right where they live. I especially want to work with families with children, so the children can learn that it is possible to grow healthy food right on their own property. To me gardening is a family project. It is good therapy; there is some kind of unity there.

People should never look at gardening as a waste of time because as much time as we put into the garden, we get out so much more: not only in fruit and vegetables, but in the feeling of being loved, the warmth and sense of accomplishment, the feeling that you're needed and what you do is appreciated.

It's as if time doesn't exist when you're in a garden. You work in the hot morning sun and the afternoon sun and the evening sun and then comes the cool breeze of night, and you still don't want to go inside. You still want to enjoy every stage of it. You look at the clock and say, "Where did all these hours go?"

Charles Robinson next to one of the many large oleander bushes in his garden.

Charles Robinson
HARVESTING PLEASURE

Visiting Charles Robinson's garden on the southernmost edge of San Diego is like coming upon a green island oasis in a gray urban sea. His infatuation with plants began when he was a child and has continued unabated. Most of his two-acre lot is devoted to fruit and vegetable growing, but he has a passion for ferns and orchids as well, and keeps exploring new horticultural territory. Now retired from the San Diego Fire Department, he finds his major frustration is that the day still is not long enough for all the gardening he would like to do.

My first real recollection of being interested in plants was before the first grade. My mother sent me to the store to get some beans. I bought the bag of beans, and as I was coming home, I dropped it. The bag broke and beans spilled all over the sidewalk. My mother, of course, told me to pick them up, but I missed some. In the next few days it rained, and those beans began to sprout, and I began to move those beans all around the yard. I'd dig them up one day and take them to one place, and the next day I'd dig them up and put them in another place.

I believe that was my very first contact with plants. Since then, I've just been fascinated with them. I call myself a "plant junkie" because I go around and collect plants like some people collect junk. I just love any kind of plant. Ever since I was a little kid, that is always the way it has been.

There have also been times in my life when it was important to be involved with plants because we had to eat. When I was a kid, we had a vegetable garden, and it was my job as a youngster to take care of it. Later, when I lived with my grandparents, they had kind of a farm, and I was always out there with my grandfather in the corn and the peas and whatever else he was growing. I can remember my grandmother having tall, beautiful gladiolas that I used to play in. That name was really fascinating to me—Gladiola!

I was born in San Diego and have lived here all my life, except for the time I spent in the service. When my wife and I were first married, we lived in a little house on Pardee Street that had a big yard. Fortunately, the man who lived two doors away from me, a retired army officer, had a big garden. He introduced me to dahlias and gave me dahlia bulbs every year. I really got deep into dahlias, and I bought bulbs from everywhere, including Holland. I got into the Dahlia Society and was really dahlia crazy for several years. I only had a small vegetable garden on the side; greens and beans were about all I grew.

From dahlias I went to chrysanthemums. I built a big green-house and started raising them, and then I got into fuchsias, and then a few ferns. Finally, I discovered staghorn ferns, and oh, gosh, I went wild with those for a while. And then I had a big patch of gladiolas for a long time. I kind of got away from the dahlias because no one would ever buy them. In 1978, we moved into this house and have almost two acres. I turned the lawn into an orchard because lawns take a lot of water and water is scarce here. Right now I've achieved probably the maximum, a nice place where I can collect all the plants I like, because I keep on finding new ones that I want.

One day I ran into a lady who asked me if I ever grew orchids. She gave me fourteen plants and that's how I got started in cymbidium orchids. I now probably have more than four hundred. So I just keep moving from one thing to another. Every so often there's something else that comes along. Right now I'm learning how to grow ferns from spores, and the latest thing I'm really excited about is bananas; I'm raising seven different varieties, and they're fruiting fairly well.

I'm also headed toward the rare and unusual fruit trees; I just got some cherimoya trees, and a Fuyu persimmon tree. A lot of people from Asia like this fruit, so that creates a little demand. I want to get into things that I like to eat, and I give away food to people in our church, as well.

I sell a little, too, because that helps pay the water bill. I sell the avocados in a bookstore in Paradise Valley, and I sell orchids to the Paradise Valley Hospital Gift Shop. I also sell sweet potatoes, and other than that, people just come by for what they want. It's been a real fine social thing for me because I get to meet so many nice people by word of mouth.

Last year, I bought six hundred slips of sweet potatoes from a commercial grower in Livingston, California, and got about 2,500 pounds from that whole plot. I wrote the grower when I ordered slips this year and told him the size of the plot. He said I was probably the champion grower in California because I was getting about twice the usual harvest. "You're doing something right," he said, and I was real happy with that. I also grow corn and tomatoes and okra, as well as peanuts, as we like to eat them.

I keep chickens for their eggs as well as for fertilizer. We have churches on both sides of our lot and no close neighbors, so no one complains about my chickens. I have a black rabbit that was a gift to my daughter, and then a white rabbit came when children of another family wanted to get rid of it. Some kids had a duck which they gave to me, but if I let him out, my four dogs will go crazy and start chasing him. I don't know what they'll do to the geese I'm about to get to help control the weeds and snails.

I guess you'd say I'm semi-organic. I keep compost and utilize all my leaves and all that. I wish I could be totally organic like some of the bio-dynamic gardeners, but I can't quite do it here. I do use fertilizers on the sweet potatoes, and I do use insecticides when I can't get rid of the bugs. I'm trying real hard to get away from it, but there are times when I just have to go with it.

I was a firefighter for thirty years, and I really liked the twenty-four-hour shift, twenty-four hours on and twenty-four hours off. My wife and kids were gone during the day and I could work all day in the garden at my own speed. Later, when I changed jobs within the department, I would hurry home and get to work in the garden in the evening and all weekend. It was just my way of relaxation. This has always been a tremendous outlet; it's been second nature to me.

My wife and I had two daughters. One daughter died of lupus two years ago. She really liked fruit, and I used to raise strawberries and apricots for her. Our other daughter got married last year; she's not too interested in gardening. My wife likes to go out and cut roses for the house, and she helps me harvest and sell, but she doesn't enjoy working in the garden very much either. When she was a kid in Louisiana, she had to work in the fields and didn't like it, so she doesn't care much for it now. But she is planning on retiring pretty soon and might change her mind when she has more time.

A field of newly planted sweet potatoes; in the distance is a small fruit orchard, one of several on his two-acre lot.

Charles has two large greenhouses on his property. His fern and orchid greenhouse has a wonderful tropical quality.

I've always gardened by myself and just like to do things myself. Our children weren't interested. For a while a niece and nephew helped me a little bit, but they would only want to help when they were right next to me. When we were picking berries off the bush, they would want to pick right where I was picking. I never could give them a job and go away and have them do it.

Sometimes they would try to help, but didn't know how. I used to debud the dahlias; dahlias have three flower buds and if you take the two off on either side, the one in the center does better. My nephew used to watch me, and every once in a while when I'd come home *all* the buds would be off the dahlias. He thought he was doing me a favor! So little things like that don't encourage me to have other people work with me. My son-in-law comes by and wants to help, but I don't know if he knows what to do or how to do it. I don't know how to train people to work with me in a garden.

Most of the things I do out here require a lot of manual labor. I think that's what I like. Take sweet potatoes. It's hard to plant them. I have to crawl around on my knees, and it is a hard job to harvest them because I have to dig them up. I say to myself, "Why do I do this? Why don't I get some easy plants?" Last night, I was out until dark planting sweet potatoes. I like to plant them in the evening so they'll have all night to recover before the sun comes up. When I came in, I was really tired, but somehow all the work is interesting to me. I enjoy every bit of it. Seems like the harder it is, the better I like it.

The anticipation of having a good crop is always there. When I see the corn coming up and I'm watching those ears develop, I'm tempted to pull back those husks and see what's inside. That's the exciting part. Same with sweet potatoes. People ask me, "When do you know the sweet potatoes are ripe?" I say, "Well, you just pull the vines back and if you see the ground cracking open, you know that something is happening down there." When I see that, it is really exciting because until then, you never know if all the things you did were right. There are so many things that can happen, or go wrong.

I went to Cuyamaca College and took a class in drip and sprinkler irrigation, specifically so that I could put in my own irrigation system. I learned how to do it, and put my orchard and sweet potatoes and corn and tomatoes on a drip system, but I haven't done it everywhere. I had to admit to myself a few days ago that I like to water. I really enjoy being out there, looking at the plants, checking each one of them to make sure they're getting enough water. It's the closeness of being with them and seeing the progress of everything going on.

I have names for some of my plants, like the big staghorn fern I call the "Big Guy." I don't exactly talk to the plants, but I say things, like, "There's my big fellah." A kind of communication goes on, not necessarily in words. I think the communication is just in being there and caressing, or you might say grooming them. That's important. I've read some fantastic articles about plants being able to sense things. I don't know, there may be something to it.

The propagation of plants is really fascinating to me. I'm doing a little grafting now, and have an apricot tree with four grafts on it from different trees. And I find seeds all the time. I love to see them grow, to watch them break out of the ground, just to see life going on. And then, of course, there are the added benefits we get from plants. We couldn't live without them. We tend to forget that.

I really enjoy *any* kind of plant. When people say, "I've got some old plants that I'm going to throw away," I say, "Don't throw them away, give them to me. I'll take care of them." I don't turn down any plant. Sometimes they live and sometimes they don't.

I've been at it for a long time now. I really enjoy every minute of it, every day of it. It's a lot of fun for me. I just don't think I am going to live long enough to do all the things I want. I'm getting older, I'm getting slower, and things are not going as fast as I would like them to go. I don't have the money to do all the things that I'd like to do. And then I begin to think, well, probably nobody does, so why should I be concerned? If I had all the money I wanted, and could buy all the equipment I wanted, and have the big orchard that I want, then what? I probably wouldn't have time for the ferns and orchids. So I say, "Aw, forget about that. I'll go ahead and enjoy what I'm doing right now."

The Garden as Teacher

Art Combe in his melon patch, where he continues to grow descendants of watermelon seed discovered in an Apache cave.

Art Combe
DESERT HORTICULTURIST

Art Combe lives in a remote valley in northwest Arizona, in a tiny town called Littlefield. There he has created an exceptional nursery specializing in nuts, cacti, and desert plants. A self-taught master horticulturalist, for over sixty years he has been developing new varieties of grains, melons, flowers, and fruit and nut trees—among them the Dehn, Utah, and Northland almonds. Now in his late eighties, Art continues to develop desert wildflowers and new fruit and nut tree varieties that he feels will be needed in the twenty-first century.

A small portion of Art's extensive cacti garden, displaying some of the cacti he has been collecting for more than forty years.

I go to bed at nine o'clock, with the chickens, and I'm up every morning at three. I prepare the food I'm going to eat for the day and do my housework, as I've never been able to train my little dog J.J. to do it. That's when I take care of my correspondence, and read my various garden, fruit, and nut-growing magazines. Very rarely am I ever interrupted this time of the morning. I can work undisturbed until the sun comes up, when I go out to work. I just can't wait to check seed that should be emerging or to visit various blooms that have appeared since the previous visit. I work every day but Sunday. Time is a precious commodity; once lost, it's lost forever!

I grew up on a farm near Ogden, Utah. My grandfather and my folks had gardened because they lived way out in the country; it was miles and miles to a store. We ate what we had on hand besides producing all the nuts and fruits. My dad didn't particularly like gardening, as he was a dairyman, but my grandfather started a nursery in 1870, and I'd tag along, always interested in what he was doing. He budded and grafted and showed me how to do that, and how to cross closely related plants. He got me interested in plants, really.

Then about 1914, our local newspaper carried a weekly column that Luther Burbank wrote, discussing plant breeding and his methods of improving plants. The articles so intrigued me that I began going to the library and borrowing books on botany and plant improvement. Burbank's philosophy and theories held me spellbound; he became a hero of mine. When one of my younger brothers was born, I persuaded my parents to name him Luther!

I first got interested in melons when I taught horticulture to the Apache Indians in White River, Arizona, from 1928 to 1930. I was looking through old caves with my students and found some red watermelon seed up Diamond Creek, within about twenty miles of White River. In a cave on a natural rock ledge, I saw a little woven basket about four or five inches high made out of split willow that had been dipped in pitch, with a cork in the top. I looked inside and even though I had never seen red watermelon seeds before, I recognized them from their shape. I figured, if the Indians could grow them in desert country, I could do as well where there was fifteen to eighteen inches of annual rain. I started growing them in 1931, and have continued to grow them ever since because their taste is delicious. The shapes of the melons were very bad, but after all these years I've got them with a good form now.

The seed that I found might have been fifty or one hundred years old. Being kept in a cool dark cave like that would produce nearly ideal conditions for preserving seed: a uniform temperature of about fifty-five degrees. I saved some of that seed for forty years and then planted it, and the germination rate was still fairly good. Just in 1987, I sent some to the seed bank at the University of Arizona so that they can preserve it.

I farmed up near Ogden, Utah, specializing in melons, but I also grew fruit and nut trees. Almost forty years ago, I moved to Littlefield, Arizona, after I retired from the farming and nursery business and turned everything over to my son in northern Utah; now he has retired and has turned over The Valley Nursery to his two sons.

Perhaps one of the reasons I decided to settle in Littlefield was the wonderful people who live here. When I first came here, there was only a trading post, a school, a post office, and about half a dozen farms; several grew vegetables commercially. Whenever I went after my mail, one farmer or the other would give me vegetables that were in season.

I converted an old school bus into a place to live by removing all the seats and installing the conveniences of a modern trailer. For a while I had permission to park the school bus under large cotton-wood trees right beside the Beaver Dam Creek, where the fishing was very good. Then I met the Walters, who ran a trading post and gas station on old Highway 91. We became very good friends, and I moved my bus up to their place.

I tried to help them as much as I could in return for all their kindness to me. One day some surveyors came; it was only then that I learned the Walters were giving me land north of their trading post. I protested, but their minds were made up. A few days later, they handed me the deed to the place where my home and cacti gardens are now.

I spent many glorious days hunting plants and prospecting, because the uranium boom was on at that time. I learned to love the unspoiled beauty of this part of the country. Every canyon, dry wash, mountain, and desert has its own beauty and differs one from another. The plant life and cacti were most interesting and different from anywhere I had lived previously, as this area is the only place in the United States where the Mohave, Sonoran, and Great Basin Deserts meet.

I cleared the desert bush off the land the Walters gave me and planted cacti, desert shrubs, trees, and fruit and nut trees. I got a permit from the Bureau of Land Management to collect any plants or cacti I wanted, but only three of each variety. This gave me an opportunity to add to the plant and cacti garden I had started years earlier near my nursery in Uintah, Utah.

I had outstanding fruit. People would come and say, "We want some of this and that," that they couldn't buy anywhere else. So I started doing it for the friends who wanted it, and it just grew. That's why I developed a seedless pomegranate; friends wanted sweet juice without the bother of seeds. Pomegranates are very high in vitamins and minerals, higher even than apple juice. Someday someone will be planting them by the thousands and selling the juice.

I also decided to experiment with pistachios to see if they'd do well here. About thirty years ago, I got some seed and budwood from a Dr. Anderson at the University of California and put in my first orchard. When I saw how well they did, I put a second one in about ten years later. Pistachios are just like a peach tree in that they must have a certain amount of cold to break their dormancy, but too much cold kills them. Here we have a little frost every winter, so this is a perfect climate for them.

This is the second nursery business I've started, and my son and daughter have moved down here to help me. I'm past eighty-five, and there is much to be done. It may be years before I retire again.

This nursery specializes in desert orchids and cacti, which I've been collecting for the last fifty years. I'm trying to develop some of the native plants so that people can have less water-intensive gardens. The time will come when people will have to plant them. Nine-tenths of families don't have the time to lie on their lawns anyway. In the future, many people will just have colored rock for their lawn and plants in between.

That's why I've done so much work on the desert orchid, because of the small amount of water it takes. The desert orchids were here thousands of years before the Indians or white men came, and had adapted against all their enemies and diseases. They're disease-free in their own environment. They grow all over seven southwestern states, clear up into Zion National Park, and bloom

Art's pistachio trees also serve as greenhouses, protecting the plants underneath from the harsh desert sun and wind.

Chilopsis linearis,
*a desert orchid which
Art is developing for
home garden use.*

from April to November. Even in the worst heat of summer, they bloom well.

But you don't see them with flowers anywhere near as big as I have developed. I've already developed a pure white one. I'm trying right now to get a blossom with a purple that extends over the entire bell. I've also found one with minimum seed pods, and I think I've found one that produces no pods at all. Ordinarily they are heavy producers of seed, and of course that saps their strength. If I get three out of these thousands that are here, I'll be happy.

We're working with other wildflowers, too. We've taken the wild desert globemallow you see mile after mile along the roadside, and have them in white, orange, and red, with much bigger flowers. Right now we're working for dwarf types, with big blooms on a dwarf plant. People have smaller gardens and like smaller plants with lots of flowers.

We've got a lot of mutations to study everywhere around here from the atomic bombs that were exploded aboveground in the 1950s. Most of the testing was done when the prevailing winds were coming this way. If the wind would change and blow toward Las Vegas, the test would be postponed. I was lucky to miss much of the fallout from the testing as I was helping my son at the nursery in northern Utah.

In many instances, the mutations are not stable. I've observed many cacti to have mutated several times. Periodically, I check the various mutations, cut off those not like the mother plant, and propagate them just to see what happens.

Even if there weren't mutations to study, there are plants to be found here that have not yet been identified. We're just that remote. The plants that are here, very few people are interested in. I could spend day after day in these hills looking for them, but I don't have the time now. I'm tied down here to the nursery.

I'm a vegetarian by necessity because it's so convenient to grow all my own food. My wife has been in a rest home for more than thirty years—just one of those things—so I live out of my garden. When you live out of your garden there mustn't be any period without something to eat, so I don't stop for a minute. As soon as I take out one crop, I put another in. Every row has got to count. If there is some plant that doesn't do too well, or looks like a nematode got into it or something, then I don't replant that same vegetable there. I move to another part of the garden.

I put up the decorations to keep the birds away, and change them every two or three days because the birds get used to the same ones, and get on to you. I have several roadrunners that are worth their weight in gold. Seldom do I ever spray for insects, as the roadrunners go up and down the rows of plants, searching for insects on the underside of the leaves. They are unafraid of me, and we work in the garden together. They have very sharp eyesight. Many times I see them fly ten to fifteen feet off the ground to catch a grasshopper that may be hidden in a tree.

I use pesticides only as a last resort. If I detect aphids and there are not enough ladybugs to control them, then I spray. I watch for and hand pick squash bugs or cucumber beetles, and that, as a rule, controls them. I have plenty of garden area and at times, I will not plant an area for six months to a year, to give it a rest. I do control all weeds that may start there.

I do use chemical fertilizers, mostly ammonium sulphate—21 percent nitrogen at the rate of five to seven pounds per 1000 square feet of garden. I apply it on top of the compost that is about two inches thick. Then, using a rototiller, I work the fertilizer and compost into the garden area, tilling four to five inches deep. All through the growing season, I side-dress with ammonium sulphate to any row that requires it. I start when the vegetables are about two inches high, making a furrow with a hoe about two inches deep on the opposite side where the drip line is laid. A handful will do five to six feet of row. Then I cover the fertilizer with soil and irrigate.

I water everything with drip irrigation, buried about two or three inches down. It cuts down on the weeds because the only place where there is water, under the plants, it is too shady for weeds to grow. Less water is wasted or lost to evaporation this way, too.

Art's vegetable garden is watered by hose buried two inches underground to conserve water.

You'll notice that underneath every pistachio and persimmon and pomegranate tree there is compost piled high around it. I brought worms up here from down along the river. I feed the angleworms and keep them fat and sassy. They take care of the compost and eat it down. As they do that, they bore holes into the ground and aerate the soil, so the water goes down well. Their manure, I figure, is just as good or better than any other animal manure.

Years ago, seeds used to cost five and ten cents a package. Now they cost a lot more, but they put less and less seed in all the time. I'm fearful that maybe it will end up with just a picture on the package and no seed inside, so I save my own seed. I save seed only from the best plants that I have marked in my garden, and only if they have been isolated from other plants that might accidentally cross-pollenize with them.

I'm ever alert for variations as I go about caring for my plants. When I do find one, I mark the plant and observe it to see if it is a mutation or throwback to one of its parents. One can only find that out by planting the seed. If it is a mutation, it will reproduce true, but if it is a throwback, the resulting seedlings will vary. If some seem worthy, they may be bagged to protect them from other pollen and the seed saved. I can know their future possibilities through the size and thickness of the leaf and how close together the leaves are. Each

114

It is startling to see cacti grown in neat rows, but the technique works well for these and other native plants.

year I select the type of plant I want, and when it comes true to what I expected, the process has been completed.

You can also make a plant vary by crossing it with a closely related variety, and then bagging the flower after pollenizing it. By the second or third generations you will note plenty of variations. If you're a good judge, you can pick out those that have possibilities: color, size, immunity to disease, or whatnot. You select the ones you like best, and each year repeat them; in seven years you have the plant coming true.

One thing I have thought of: as a plant is, it was also once before. If a plant is uniform, cross it with anything that's related to it and you upset it. You throw it back to what it has been and what it may be in the future. For example, I found a desert globemallow that had a little bit of pink in it and I crossed it with an orange one. Lo and behold, in the second generation a pretty good red came up. There must have been a time in history that favored plants with red petals; maybe an insect that was attracted to red plants moved into that area.

Each year I have students from different schools come to study my gardens and the work I am doing. Out of every group of thirty or forty or fifty, there are always two or three that are inquisitive. They'll come back time and time again. The knowledge they're gaining will perpetuate itself, just like the plants they're working with. It makes me feel good that what I'm doing will not be lost.

The kids getting out of school now were born in one of the greatest times in all history. The good farmland is shrinking as land has become too expensive to farm on account of taxes. The choice land is being taken over by developers for homes and business sites. It will be a challenge to these young people to create higher-producing and disease-resistant plants to feed a hungry world. Look at the possibilities—they're endless. There is not a plant on earth which has reached perfection, or can't be improved. It doesn't matter if it's grains or potatoes or flowers or fruit trees. If you stop a minute, you fall behind!

To tell you the truth, I love plants, just like I do people. I enjoy tending them. Many of my choice plants, which I call my pets, have been given to me by friends. Each time I water or prune them, I think of the person that gave them to me. It feels like renewing an old friendship, and leaves me with pleasant memories.

As I work I talk to myself and to them. I realize they don't understand me, but I do think they understand and appreciate good care. Look at some of your friends. How many starts can you give them and they never get anything to grow? I think if they loved the plants, they'd do better for them.

I keep track of everything I've done mostly in my mind, but since 1965, I've been writing a page a day on what I'm doing and working with, to keep track of my experiments. My mind never stops for a minute. No matter what I'm working with, I'll be thinking of all the possibilities or what I can do with it. Like I just said, there is not a plant that stands still if you guide it right. I ought to put down more of my theories so that the universities can either make a liar of me or prove that I'm right. I've had so many professors come here and say, "Do you write these things down?" I say, "No, if I wrote them down, I wouldn't have time to do anything!" They usually get a bang out of that.

A lot of people like murder mysteries. I have the same feeling, only I like to unravel the mysteries of plants. I just love matching wits with them. It's a challenge. The mystery's there; I'll just keep at it to find out all about it. It gives me something to live for. I could never hope to get it all done, but the possibilities are tremendous.

Mike Sacco, pausing for a moment along Interstate 90 in Spokane.

Mike Sacco
GARDENING EN ROUTE

How many people enter and exit their workplace at fifty-five miles per hour? Mike Sacco does every day as he tends a stretch of freeway planting in the heart of Spokane, Washington. Many of us take highway landscaping and maintenance for granted, seldom imagining how bleak and unsightly our cities would be without people like Mike. He came to highway landscaping and maintenance through a circuitous route, but gardening has always been important to him and his family. He knows how much freeway planting contributes to a city and its quality of life, and has come to enjoy the special rewards and hazards of this work.

*F*reeway planting has its own challenges. There is often restricted soil volume and depth in a narrow corridor with pavement on both sides. Ninety degree temperatures in the summer are typical here, and minus twenty in the winter is not uncommon. There is extra heat from the heat absorption of the pavement, and greater extremes of temperature. Strong winds are created especially during the rush hour by the traffic, and particularly truck traffic. There are all the little microenvironments with their attendant insect and rodent populations, and we have to determine how to control these.

There are errant motorists who occasionally crash into the area. We also have special problems in the small triangular pieces of land where everything sharpens down to a point at each entry and exit ramp. A lot of cars run across them, especially in the winter when the roads are slick. We do our best to keep the roads plowed in the wintertime, and sometimes it seems like motorists do their best to run off the road.

When we plow in the wintertime, the salt and other chemicals that we use to clear the ice off the roadway get dumped onto the soils along with the snow. I lost 350 new plants one winter because the snow did not melt from week to week. As each snowfall was plowed, it built up, so the plants were buried in urea-ladened snow. They just got fried, so we're no longer using urea.

All of the fifty acres plus along Interstate 90 between milepost 282 and 279, and the rest areas at either end of town, are my responsibility. The traffic volume here is higher than about anywhere else in the city. When I came to this department, this particular area was pretty bare, and the prevailing wisdom was that nothing could grow here because of the salt damage and intense heat.

The plan I developed for everything planted in this particular half-mile-long corridor was for good fall color. We added more ivy and Virginia creeper and burning bush (dwarf winged euonymus) and a couple of different varieties of viburnum. The columnare maples have done all right, but not the vine maples; that experiment failed, as they were stressed. We'll replace those with Peking cotoneaster; they should probably do all right. In five years, when all these young plants planted over the last two years mature, this should be a premiere fall color spot in Spokane. I'm really excited about that because it's my shot at creativity; I had this whole blank slate to work with, a mile of bare ground.

This section of freeway is about seventeen or eighteen years old, and much of the planting in other areas was done when the freeway was completed. It is starting to look a little tattered now, and will need some refurbishing, as will its irrigation system. Our lawn and landscaped areas are just about equally divided into twenty-five acres of lawn and twenty-seven acres or so of landscaping. The lawn is a little more difficult to maintain than the landscaped areas because there we use low maintenance varieties of shrubs and trees and ground covers. Why we have so much lawn, I really don't know. That was the choice of the landscape architect, perhaps because Spokane is a gardening town.

That's a tremendous plus for a city. In any neighborhood, I don't care what part of town, it is unusual to see yards and lawns not well kept. Lawns are still the single biggest feature in most yards, and so my guess is that it reflects Spokane's gardening principles.

Probably another reason why people continue to garden here is the rich heritage of Spokane's public parks. They tend to set the tone of a city. Some of our parks were designed by well-known landscape architects. Manito Park has a formal garden that is unsurpassed, and a beautiful Japanese garden, and their rose garden and perennial beds are beautiful, too. The outlying parks are older but have been very well maintained through the years.

I think our park system does more with less than about anybody I can imagine. It's always very easy to criticize government agencies and employees, but I've seen what they do, and I know what they have to work with. The job they do is absolutely amazing.

There are times I'd like to go to city council meetings and shake people when it comes to budget time, because, of course, the budget of the Park Department is always one of the first to be cut. I just want to grab them and say, "Do you know what kind of a heritage you're throwing away here?" I guess others feel as I do though, for the city recently passed two park bond issues. I'm the only permanent employee with the Department of Transportation, Highway Division, assigned to landscaping. I'm a Maintenance Tech II, and technically my job does not differ from anyone else who works for the highway department who does roadside work, which includes patching and fixing guardrail, chain link fence, and all those other things. It just happened that my background was landscaping and they needed someone to fill that position.

There is also only one permanent employee assigned to the irrigation of all this. You can imagine what kind of job that is. There are miles and miles of pipeline and thousands of sprinklers. Neither one of us can keep up, and as you look around, it's obvious. The

Pfitzer juniper forms a sturdy and dense ground cover along the freeway and surrounds the Bechtel prairie crabapple trees growing in containers.

large brown area of paxistima on a south-facing slope was caused by one failed sprinkler head during a four-day period of ninety degree heat. You can see other areas that need attention, but we just can't be everywhere at once. We do get seasonal help in the form of temporary employees, but they're always unskilled and often don't have any background in gardening.

As I mentioned before, we choose our materials to be low maintenance: drought, disease, and insect resistant. You'll see very little along our freeway that requires a lot of water. But in my mind the term *low maintenance* is something of a joke. There really is no such thing. Certainly what we do costs much less to maintain than a flower garden. But every plant needs some kind of care, and there is still a tremendous amount of work to do. To have one person taking care of fifty acres with a handful of unskilled labor is taxing.

If the public knew how many of their tax dollars are going towards just picking up litter, it would stagger them. And they would stop littering because it *is* costing them money. We have to send out two people twice a week to pick up litter just on this short section of the freeway. Multiply that by the interstate that goes across the whole country, plus all the other state roads that interweave, and the cost is just ridiculous.

120

Everything here was designed by a landscape architect who works for us. The only time I get involved in design work is when a large planting has died out for some reason or another, and then I come up with a design and choose the plant materials. Then, of course, it has to be okayed by the architect and our horticulturist in Olympia. I feel lucky that our maintenance administrator has committed himself to keeping this landscape looking nice. He feels if we have it, it should be done right, and that's the way I feel, too, as a taxpayer as well. But in the past, some administrators didn't want any landscaping at all and wouldn't fund any real maintenance for it.

Our architect has come up with many nice designs. Throughout our whole landscape we're repeating redleaf barberry for accent, specimen trees in concrete pots, abundant use of pfitzer, Sargent, and tam junipers, European mountain ash, Japanese flowering crabapple, Ponderosa and Austrian black pine, ivy cascading down walls, and Virginia creeper on some of the fences for accent and as a noise and sight barrier. The chain link fences that we are required by law to put around every area to keep animals and people out always spoil the look a little for me, but it's something you learn to live with.

Spokane is a semiarid region, so everything we have is heavily irrigated. We are in our fourth straight year of below normal rainfall. Even native plants are getting stressed. We're seeing native pine trees that seemingly require no watering start to lose their second- and third-year needles.

We don't spray insecticides or fungicides; those things are contracted. The liability is very high on those kinds of pesticides, and we leave it to people who do that solely for their living. But I could not do the job I do without herbicides. We use a fall-applied herbicide which is a preemergent; it takes care of weeds before they emerge from the ground. We use that every year, and every few years we have to give it a rest because it will build up a residue in the ground. But it's been a lifesaver. Before I came here, the landscape program was basically a weed control program. With a crew of maybe six temporary employees, we would do nothing but hand-pull weeds from one end of the freeway to the other.

Because this is public land, however, we have to use extreme caution, both for the public's protection and our own. If I take a little spray bottle of Trimec, for instance, and spray one dandelion, I have to fill out a spray record. Because we're a public agency, we have to have very accurate and thorough record-keeping, which works to everyone's advantage.

I got into freeway planting accidentally. About ten years ago, I was a state employee with the Department of Social and Health Services, working with retarded children. It just happened that a promotion came up as a highway landscape caretaker. I had been gardening at home for quite some time and had done landscaping as a civilian employee at an airbase. I subsequently became involved with the Master Gardener program, and then this opportunity for promotion opened up here.

I'm proud of what I'm doing. When you have worked hard for a whole day, you can look back and say, "Gee, that looks better. I did that." It is very satisfying to drive along a freeway and know that you've contributed to making your city more beautiful and, therefore, more habitable.

I'm sure that's a lot of why I continue to do this, the gratification I get from being able to improve an area and being acknowledged for that. In the five years that I've been here, there has been some noticeable improvement. We've gotten some feedback from the general public and the professional community that what we're doing here is noticed. This is a highly visible area that everyone in Spokane sees. It increases civic pride to make the city more beautiful, and for a lot of people who only pass through Spokane, this may be all they see of the whole city.

Gardening has taught me that nothing stays the same. What you're working with is vital, and if a plant stops growing, it starts to die. I have to continually remind people that what we're dealing with here is not like road service work, where if we don't get to this paving project now, we can get to it next September. With landscaping, you must get to it in its own time, or it's too late.

But the fact that it's always changing reminds me that I have to be flexible. I can't hold to a schedule that is fixed; I have to work according to the needs of my charges, the shrubs, trees, and turf. And I've become a weatherwatcher since I've become a landscaper because we have to constantly adjust our irrigation system to it. I suppose, as a person, I tend to be a little inflexible, so this is probably the best thing I could be doing; it's constant training in being able to go with whatever is happening.

I come from a gardening family. My grandmother was the first generation to arrive here from Calabria, in the southern part of Italy, where she had worked in her father's vineyard. One of the ways she learned English was by listening to an old radio show about gardening sponsored by Shell Oil. She was a wonderful gardener and had the richest soil. She'd never think of using an herbicide; she dug dandelions out of her yard with a paring knife. If somebody gave her roses for her birthday, she'd take a cut rose and plant it in her rose garden without the aid of any rooting hormone, covering it with a quart jar that was lined with dirt. By God, it was a rosebush the next season, and it continued to survive. Nowadays, you can't find a rose that isn't grafted to a wildrose root stock.

I stayed with her quite a bit when I was young. When I was ten, she gave me my first tree to grow for myself. When she passed away, there was a whole lifetime of her things to be divided up among family members, but I wasn't interested in her furniture or knickknacks or anything like that. I dug up three rosebushes from her garden.

I suppose one of the reasons that I continue to do landscaping is because this work is very respected in my family. My children tell their friends when they drive along the freeway on a field trip in the school bus, "This is my dad's office." My parents are both avid gardeners. They have a very beautiful yard; in fact, my wife and I were married in their back garden. My aunts and uncles are all vegetable gardeners and have nice yards. They really work at it; it's a matter of pride with them. My wife also likes to garden, and in fact she's the main gardener at home because, when I come home after eight hours of working in the soil, the last thing I feel like doing is pruning or taking care of the lawn.

I don't think beautification is ever a waste of time, especially in today's world, and that's the essence of landscaping. I really enjoy pruning trees and shrubs, knowing that when I make a cut on a tree, I'm not making it solely for the beauty of that tree right now, I'm guiding the direction and growth of that tree for the next five or ten years. I get a lot of enjoyment out of that side of my work, the art side, and I really enjoy the science side as well.

I rely heavily on the research that's done at land grant colleges. For example, it used to be standard to amend the soil around a plant when putting it in the ground. But we don't do that anymore because they've discovered that you're just enlarging the pot the plant came in by that nearly perfect soil. Often the roots don't try to escape and grow into the native soil, so, as the foliage continues to grow, you get five-dollar foliage on a one-dollar root system. In not too long a time, the plant may outgrow its root system and die, wasting a lot of labor as well as money.

But of course, some plants do well in amended soil, and some plants do well even when you've gone against all the scientifically accepted horticultural practices. Something else is at work in that area of gardening, beyond or beside the science of it, in understanding why things grow. I couldn't put a name to what that something else is, but that's one of the reasons I'm in gardening. It's the combination of the person, the plant, and the environment. I guess if I wanted to take it to a real extreme, I would say that there's definitely a mystical aspect to gardening.

I remember in the early seventies a book came out about how playing music to your houseplants brought positive results. I asked my grandmother in kind of a joking way if she talked to her plants, and she said, "Of course." So then I paid attention to what she did; she didn't talk so much as she sang, but it was a kind of speak-singing, in Italian.

I can't say what it was she was saying to them, or what she heard back. But I do know that when I first started to prune, I was very tentative and wondered, should I take this branch off or shouldn't I? Now I approach a tree with a lot more confidence. But on the occasions when I do get stuck, I just ask the tree. I literally ask, "Should I be taking this?" And I always feel very right about taking the limb or feel that I should leave it. It's always a very definite, strong feeling. It's nothing particularly emotional, I just know what to do.

I don't think that there's any doubt that there is something going on between plant life and people, and for some reason it seems to be particularly strong with trees for me. I really value the contributions the landscape architect in his office makes, or the scientist in his lab, but I think they miss a lot by not being in the field. They're too far removed from the reality of plant life.

I think a great many people who work outside, whether professionally or in their home gardens, do feel a kinship with what they're growing. They don't feel like they own it, and it's more than an affinity; it's a genuine kinship, one vital organism to another. I hope someday researchers and scientists will come out of their labs long enough to feel it, to realize that something's there. I'd love to see some research done. I don't think we have instruments yet that are fine enough, and subtle enough, to measure that kind of communication or kinship, but I don't have any doubt that someday we will. And then we'll rely on the scientists to, in essence, describe and define what we gardeners have been feeling for generations.

Ted Kipping surrounded by rhododendrons, pierises, abutilons, ajuga, and tree fuchsia.

Ted Kipping
A TERMINAL CASE

Ted Kipping is a master horticulturist by passion, a paleo-ecologist by training, and a tree trimmer by trade. He began working with trees and plants almost by accident and discovered he couldn't live without them. His quest to learn everything he could about plants and trees has taken him all over the world. Ted's almost encyclopedic horticultural knowledge enabled him to turn living in a fog belt in San Francisco into an asset, by creating a cloud forest garden in his own backyard.

I'm a terminal case, a person whose profession became an obsession. There is an endless pool of plants to learn about, grow, make happy, and be happy from, and a seemingly endless pool of delightful people with whom to share them. That's maybe the nicest part of all, the other plant fanatics I meet all over the world.

I became a horticulturist by working at the Strybing Arboretum in Golden Gate Park. I was interested in plants at that time, but I wasn't hooked. I became aware that I was hooked when I left the park in 1973. I went into another line of work altogether—things along the line of community service—but in the meantime, I discovered I couldn't exist without plants.

And I realized that plant people were some of my favorite people anywhere, regardless of what other sterling virtues nonplant people had. Plant people tend to be, or at least the ones that are terminal cases, community oriented. They tend to have well-developed minds, although maybe they've lost them in the garden. They tend to be very personable, very giving. That may have something to do with the nature of working with plants; with seeds and cuttings you always have an embarrassing abundance of things to give away.

When I first gardened, I decided I would do just the minimum effort for the plants. I'd set them around where I wanted them and they'd either grow or not grow. Lots of them died, and that was a sobering lesson. The second time I made a little more effort for them. I mulched and even built a few raised beds for greater drainage. I still put things where I wanted them to go for the pattern, forgetting about conditions of light and shade and drainage. Well, where I made the effort, things really thrived, and where I was very arbitrary, things didn't. With my present garden, I decided to put myself "at the gentle mercy of the plants," as Hildegard Flanner said. I put about a year into the initial landscaping and three months just doing soil preparations. That was really difficult, to restrain myself from planting anything during that whole time.

Seventy-five tons of rock went in. There is probably ten tons of concrete and steel. We moved out many many tons of clay and moved in many tons of decomposed granite and leaf mold and sand. There are thirteen different soil mixes because I'm trying to give each plant what it needs. It ranges from pure gravel, pure Dillon Beach sand, pure granite grit, pure sphagnum moss, pure clay, pure duff, and then mixes in between, like sharp granite grit mixed with well-decomposed leaf mold and finely ground peat.

Western mountain plants such as alliums, buckwheats, silvery lupines, zauschnerias, grasses, and penstemons border handmade concrete steps; the steep slope beyond is devoted to succulents.

Healthy soil conditions lead to healthy plants. Bugs and diseases affect most those that are stressed. I don't describe myself as an organic gardener, although I never spray in my garden. I recommend it to my clients only with great reluctance, and with their knowing that it will change the balance of things in their garden.

To me there are two aspects of gardening, the art and the craft. The craft is making the plants happy, and the art is creating some drama so that it's interesting from different viewpoints over a long period of time. My wife and son and I live in a fog belt, so I have tried to recreate—with my friend Harlan Hand's loving assistance and eye and brain—something resembling a rocky outcrop in a cloud forest. The climate is ideal to try this.

My garden faces south, with high fences and buildings on two sides, so along the sides I planted fast-growing, canelike things: abutilons or flowering maples, cestrums, iochromas, giant salvia, tall fuchsias, and various vines, mostly things from cloud forest areas. With the misting system I put in and the soil preparations, the plants really took off, and in a year grew nine to eighteen feet, exactly what we needed to obscure these other structures.

The rest of the garden steps down quickly into smaller plants, so that we can have a greater variety and not feel quite so crowded. The bigger the leaf, the smaller the place looks. The finer the texture, the larger. There were some really neat plants that I craved for years, but when I popped them in, the whole place shrank. So I tearfully pulled them out and found them other homes.

Cloud forest plants like warm days and cool nights, so those went in, and the rest of the plants are either plants of alpine areas or tundra or cliffs or bogs. The cliff plants come from the cliffs and islands of Baja and Mexico, and the coastal cliffs of California. Some of these I collected; and others have come from friends, through trades or purchases. I suppose if you tracked down the nativity and the channels of all the plants in my garden, you'd have a complex skein of rather remarkable horticulturists and botanists from all over the world.

I thought that this would be a neat place to try alpine plants because, even though we get wet winters, if I could give them sufficient drainage, they might tolerate that. They seem to be prospering, for the most part. Some of them, instead of going through a big burst of color for three weeks or so as they might in the wild, have been giving a sparkly display of color for three or four months. There are enough different plants in my garden that it gives the sense of being in bloom all year long.

Morning sun and afternoon shade suit many small woodland and alpine plants, among them weeping hemlock, phloxes, mossy saxifrages, evening primroses, iochromas, and abutilons.

My garden's a mixture of curiosity, love, and need. It's a thing to share. I welcome people to come and compare one species or variety to another. I've got everything I can get my hands on of certain small sizes of things, just to compare them.

I played with plants as a child and saw the hills around San Francisco disappear under housing, so I tried to put a wild garden in my parents' backyard. But my folks had three kids and when we played back there with all our friends, we really tore the hell out of it. It was like having a bunch of goats in a small space. Too much of any creature, even fifty doves in a garden, is going to demolish it. That's why I don't put out bird feeders any more. I grow plants that attract birds, but only a limited number of each kind.

I went off to Columbia University to become a scientist and studied paleo-ecology, which is sort of a Sherlock Holmes game played with just faint little hints in the rocks of what the earth was like long ago. It can lead you to some pretty sobering extrapolations about how ephemeral any scene is. You watch how quickly some creatures disappear in the geological clock, and how little it takes to alter things, so it teaches you to appreciate what we have.

I wish that more people would cease to be conquistadors and start being the crew of "Spaceship Earth," because that's what we are. We're not merely passengers or spectators. We don't have a spare planet. We've got to stop doing whatever we please and saying to hell with anybody else.

Anyway, I was considering becoming a professor, but then academic politics reared its ugly head, and I realized a lot of people in universities have been in the womb too long. They need to go dig ditches for a while to get another touch of reality. They were like these little birds that were shoving each other out of the nest. They really needed to go out and fly for a while and then come back and sit in the tree and explain to the others how to fly. It's foolish to hire someone to teach a subject who has never earned his living in it.

I left the academic scene and was looking for something to do in the interim that was useful while I figured out what to do with my life. I took long walks everywhere. One day, I walked through the arboretum and realized it was a living library or museum, if you will. And I thought, I've always enjoyed gardening, so I took the test and got hired.

I started fanatically studying about horticulture, and found I really liked all sides of it, the cultivating, propagating, landscaping, and so on. I had done tree pruning before, but I learned a lot more by working with some wonderful tree men. After I left the park and had to decide what to do, I made a little chart with all my strengths and weaknesses, and what I really enjoyed doing, and they all seemed to radiate out in different directions. So I decided to find the activity that would act like a hub, so they'd be spokes of a wheel that would let me journey along rather than take me in a million directions.

I love pruning. I absolutely love it, and it seemed to be the one place where there weren't a lot of experts already established, so I could make a dent and offer something. I've been doing it now for ten years, and I'm noticing people all over the place imitating my approach to pruning. It's encouraging.

I think all the time I spent in high school drawing classes and metal and woodworking shops helped me tremendously; a sculpting class I took at Columbia was also a big help. All those things helped me to train my eye and to tune in, because when you're pruning, you're sculpting with time and the life force of that particular plant.

I have about ten people working with me. Most of them have a background in some area of the arts, are athletic, and want to be out of doors. The pruning of trees is not comfortable, so you have to be athletic enough not to put a lot of attention on your body comfort, but to actually enjoy the rigors of using your body to the limit. And you have to be enough of an artist to tune out the distractions of how uncomfortable you are, and to be willing to go through whatever grief it takes to produce a good result.

Pruning has become an obsession. If I see a tree with dead branches or rips and tears, I've got to get in there and clean it out. The more you do something, the more you get pulled to do it. Just like a dry plant calls you. If you've spent a few million hours watering plants, either you don't ever want to see another one in your lifetime, or you can't stand for one to be suffering. Any time you're responsible for the well-being of another creature, a really wonderful thing happens: you increase your ability to respond. You can feel what is going on with plants, too, if you pay attention, just like with people or anything else. And one joy of going back to the same plants year after year is the opportunity to learn from them. Plants continually surprise me.

Trees certainly respond to the way they are pruned, not just what is done to them but how it is done to them. Some of the people who have worked alongside me have had a horrible attitude. Some of them should just be kept away from sharp instruments because their emotional state is very tough on the plants. Those plants didn't grow

Lupines, wallflowers, daisies, wild buckwheats, and brodiaeas give way to a pond surrounded by moisture-loving plants.

very much after that. They don't want to be punished again. Anyone could see the difference within the next season.

The spirits of plants really do vary. Some are very vegetative, if you will. Some are very powerful; their psychic decibels are louder and more powerful than others. It's the same with trees. I've been in some trees that I have trimmed that I have awakened, and there have been some trees that have awakened me. Have you ever rubbed the chest of some big old heavy dog, and your hand's tired and you're ready to quit, but the dog grabs your hand, shoves it back, and you know you can't stop yet? Well, there have been times when my body has been hungry and tired and I thought I would quit, when the tree goes, "There's a bunch of dead twigs left you haven't gotten yet." If I see what it was trying to tell me and start making the effort to do it, I'll get a burst of energy from the tree, a big thank-you washing back from it.

It gives me a real pleasure to prune, to see a tree cleanly groomed and dancing in its own space. I want to enhance as many trees as possible. I want to see as many appropriate trees planted as possible. I also want to see as many flowers and shrubs planted as possible. I really want to see the world beautified. That doesn't mean destroying what we've already got; sometimes it means awakening people to the potential that's already there. I want to make each thing

I do the best thing I've ever done. That makes it fun and keeps the learning curve high.

The underpinning of everything is creation, what's going on constantly. We're all experiencing, if we're right here, the pulse beat of a very complex creation that's happening right now. We're part of the creative spirit underlying everything. We can dance with it or against it or contribute to the flow of it. When we dance with it, when it's from the heart, doors open within doors and things unfold.

I have gone to lots of places in this country and around the world to study plants and gardens, and I take as many illustrative pictures as possible. It has resulted in a collection that now numbers a couple hundred thousand slides, and enables me to share as much as possible of my travels. Love of plants is a wonderful thing to infect somebody with.

Plants are a source of joy for me, an elation that takes me completely away from the cares of the world. If I'm lucky enough to get home before dark, I go tearing down into my garden to look around. The first thing I do is to see who's in bloom, and then what damage the raccoons have done, and then I may just start puttering. The time will slide away, and the next thing I know it's dark. Whatever little jagged waves there were in my day, whatever turmoil was pecking away at my foundations or spirit, just evaporate in grooming and caring for the garden and being exposed to the spirits of all those plants. Their companionship is a balm to the spirit. I consider myself more of a zoo keeper than a collector, although I'm the one nourished by my charges.

I don't think gardening is important; I'd say it's crucial. I think the more people we have gardening, whether it's to grow their own tomatoes or kiwis or just to have a pink and blue border, the more incalculable will be the return. We beautify ourselves in the process of beautifying the world; maybe that's one of the nicest spinoffs. I've noticed a real softening in myself as I've opened up to the soft strength of plants. They do their utmost at any opportunity, and it's difficult not to be affected by that.

Hazel Suedes in the ornamental greenhouse at Meadow Acres Nursery.

Hazel Suedes
NURSING CUSTOMERS AND PLANTS

Gardening in Wyoming can be more difficult than gardening in Alaska. Even though the season is approximately the same—from Memorial Day to Labor Day—Alaskans enjoy more hours of sunlight. The gardeners of Casper, Wyoming, however, have one advantage over their Alaskan counterparts— the presence of Hazel Suedes and Meadow Acres Nursery. Since she opened the nursery in 1979, Hazel has gone out of her way, both literally and metaphorically, to provide excellent horticultural and customer service. Her sales clerks even try to help customers find plants best suited to the climates in their neighborhoods. She has combined her background in nursing with a lot of very hard work to give both customers and plants an extra amount of tender loving care.

I don't know what it is about gardening that is therapeutic, but I can see people come through the door with their faces all tense, and as they walk through the greenhouse they noticeably relax. Maybe they're absorbed with color, maybe it's the increased humidity, maybe it's being away from the world of noise and gas fumes. Maybe it's just the peace and quiet and being closer to nature.

I don't know what the key is, but there is a definite psychological need. We see it, starting in the spring, when people just have to start digging in the dirt. I sometimes wonder if it doesn't have something to do with creation and our demise, from dust to dust. We started that way, we end up that way. Is there some kind of spiritual reason why we feel that affinity for the soil?

I grew up on a farm in South Dakota, and mom always gardened. I can remember zinnias and geraniums and the vegetable garden. I suppose from there came some dormant—no pun intended—desire to garden, but I didn't even realize I liked it until we moved to Casper and had to do a major overhaul on our yard.

The previous owner had done nothing to the yard for probably fourteen years, and as we worked through it all, I found I was very interested. I had just been so busy with my family and working that I never had time for gardening before. I had been in nursing all my life, and, for about fifteen years, I also taught nursing. I was a clinical instructor in the intensive care and neurological and surgical units, responsible for hospital clinical practice.

We really enjoyed our home in Casper and the yard we put in, and when we moved outside of Casper to the Evansville area, I decided I was tired of nursing stress and just wanted to be home for a while. One of our neighbors had an old greenhouse, and my husband Bob and I leased it and started growing vegetables and bedding plants for outlets in Casper.

That greenhouse turned out to be totally inadequate and too expensive to heat, so we built our own and thought we'd sell wholesale. As things have developed, we've probably become 90 percent retail; the other 10 percent is custom growing for commercial or industrial establishments, such as the Parks Department or the Country Club. I'm happy to be retail rather than wholesale because it really gives me a chance to help both the homeowner and the professional gardener.

I also do landscape consulting. I guess I do that a little differently than many people. I schedule an appointment when both the husband and wife are there, if possible, and we always start in the house, so I can see what their interior decorating is like and can talk to them a little about their likes and dislikes. I see what colors they like to live with, and see what part of their gardens they view the most, whether it is from their kitchen window or their living room window or front yard or whatever. And then I try to set something up whereby they have color or texture that greets the seasons, that they can see all through spring to fall. That way, the garden reflects them and becomes an extension of their house.

My husband and I work together in this business during the summer months, but during the rest of the year he teaches economics at Casper Community College. Our twin daughters are both in college, and to date they don't seem to be interested in the nursery business, but that's okay. They're not interested in economics or nursing either.

We're open for business the first of April through the first of October, and the background work goes on all the rest of the time. During our busy time—May and June—we have from twelve to twenty part-time employees, but only six full-time seasonal employees. I've created a lot of part-time jobs this year so that people can continue working part-time in town during the winter.

I do the selling, purchasing, propagating, landscape consulting, and garden design. In addition to running the business in general, I write all my own ads. That takes some energy! My husband does the installations in the summer and handles the books. We may soon have to open up earlier and stay open longer, but we don't want to be open year-round. We want to rejuvenate ourselves and be ready to open in the spring with enthusiasm and everything in order. When you're a customer, there's nothing worse than to have a salesclerk say, "Please leave me alone while I get this done."

In general, there is not a lot of gardening expertise in Casper because gardening conditions are so difficult. And we also have a lot of transient people because of our oil and uranium industry. People have come here from Missouri or Florida or Oregon or wherever, and they're ready to start gardening in February. They're defeated if they garden the way they did back home. Underground seed and root crops can be planted earlier, but unless people are willing to cover everything they have planted every night, they ought to wait until the last weekend in May to put in their summer garden.

Our customers want so badly to garden and have been so frustrated by what has been offered, such as Zone 6 plant material when Casper falls into Zones 3 and 4, with a little protected river

One of several tree nursery areas at Meadow Acres.

bottom pocket in North Casper that's Zone 5. So our first question to every customer is always, "Where in town do you live?" We try to get them to let us know which plants do the best in their neighborhoods.

We have such extreme temperature variations; we can go from below zero at night to way above zero the next day when a Chinook wind comes in. It's totally unpredictable, and puts our trees and shrubs and everything else under a lot of stress. Eliminating or trying to relieve some of that stress, both for the plants and their owners, is really challenging.

Our gardening season is short. We can get our first frost as early as Labor Day, and it can be cool into June, so we might have seventy frost-free days. We purchase all of our plants and seeds with that in mind. We grow all the tomatoes we sell from seed, and we don't use anything that takes over sixty-five days to mature. Early Girl is the earliest, and then we have a subarctic tomato that I believe matures in forty-five days.

We make a lot of effort to find plant stock that will survive in these conditions. We've had trouble getting in bare root stock early enough in the spring. Growers say, "But we don't send it that early." So we've gone back to the growers in other parts of the country, picked it up ourselves, put it in our lathe house, and grown it slowly. This way, when we do put it in a container, it will have an opportunity to develop a good root system and have a chance to survive. We also buy balled and burlapped trees from some of the growers, but digging them out of the ground when they are sold is very labor intensive and expensive. We have to find the right plan for us and for Casper, and we're working on it.

Of course, I've had to learn that you can't be a perfectionist and stay in this business because nature ultimately controls it all. We try our best and do all the watering and fertilizing and so forth, and still some element of nature will intervene. No matter how hard you try, there is always something else that can come along to throw you a little curve. We do have to use a lot of insecticides and chemical fertilizers in the greenhouses, but I am very cautious and respectful of those chemicals. We only utilize them enough to control the problem and be ahead of it.

Of all the things I do, watering is the thing that relaxes me most; that's why I do it. It's probably the most important job because if the water doesn't get to that little root hair, everything else that you've done is wasted. I also like watering and the feeding because it gives me time to think, and it's fun to fantasize and dream up what I'd like to do in Mr. So-and-So's garden.

I've had to teach myself everything about gardening in the Rocky Mountain area. We joined many national organizations and get their literature. We also subscribe to professional magazines, and I bought a number of the professional books. They were written in such jargon that when I first started reading them, I thought, a *hard* pinch? What's the difference between a hard pinch and a soft pinch?

I was a novice, and it was so frustrating to read some of those things. We made some phenomenal mistakes.

But then I began to approach gardening with my nursing background, which has been surprisingly helpful in this business. I started asking myself, what are the needs of this plant? What are the signs and symptoms of disease? What do you do about it? What is the preventive care for it? What is the environment it is in, and what can you expect? I have taught myself what the optimum should be in a plant's growth and development, and what the variables are that can cause problems.

I think that approach has helped greatly because the gardener and homeowner want answers to those questions, too. Generally, you can give customers pretty clear-cut answers, but there is always that unknown element: we don't really know what they'll do when they get home, or what the weather will be. Our guarantee to our customers is 50 percent of the purchase price back if they come to us during the growing season with a problem, regardless of what they put in or what they do. I think that's pretty generous.

Ours is a seasonal business, and so in January and February I can catch up on what I haven't had time to do the rest of the year. This winter I hope to have the time to draw up what in nursing are called "care sheets" on the plants we sell. These would be sheets attached to the plants telling what conditions the plant needs, if it is annual or perennial, and if perennial, how long it might live if it received good care. Since our staff is also seasonal, these sheets would help to inform them and relieve some of their anxieties about selling when customers ask them questions.

I'm also working on a gardener's calendar for this area that would tell people, for example, what they need to do for their fruit trees in mid-May or how to take care of the apple trees that have blight. Even in our ads we try not only to sell, but also to advise and educate. When our ad says, "Now is the time to . . ." it's not just hype. It actually *is* the best time to plant whatever we're advertising.

So much of our education has to be about what's under the plant. That is just as important as what goes on aboveground. If you prepare the soil environment properly, you're going to be rewarded. In addition to teaching people in general about plants, I've also been teaching about xeriscape planting, which is using drought-tolerant native grasses, shrubs, and trees to conserve water. That, combined with mulches and windbreaks, can make a real difference in water consumption. It is just common-sense gardening because our yearly rainfall averages fourteen inches, and our water has become quite expensive.

I suppose, in part because of my background in nursing, I also became a member of the Hortitherapy Society, a national organization that probably isn't ten years old yet. It was formed to provide therapy through gardening for any disadvantaged or disabled individual, whether the handicap is physical or psychological. It has been active in institutions, such as prisons, and in ghettos. The rehabilitation unit here at our hospital is beginning to start a little chapter.

Because the employment possibilities for the handicapped are so limited, we built our greenhouse sidewalks wide enough for wheelchairs. We wanted to offer some jobs here at our nursery, and had a paraplegic do all the transplanting the first year. Some employees have worked out very well, and some haven't.

I also lecture around the city to community groups, such as the Geologists Wives, the Violet Club, and the Nutritionists, who want to know about the chemicals in food and food values and that kind of thing. About two years ago, I happened to be writing a presentation for the local garden club on tissue culture roses. We'd sold a few from native plants; it was intriguing, and I was interested in it.

Rather than starting a plant from a cutting or a root, you take the growing tip of one of your best plants, making sure it is disease free. This is put in special media—agar and vitamins and such—under sterile conditions; usually it's a growth chamber so everything can be kept absolutely constant. The plant tissue makes hundreds of little clones which are then separated under sterile techniques.

This was easy for me to do because of my nursing background. A scientist from an Australian tissue culture firm was in town, and asked me to see if I could clone their violets and grow them in Casper. We found it could be done, but no one is sure if there is a demand for what they wanted to sell. I was sent to Holland recently by the Wyoming Community Development Authority to see a lab built by this same Australian firm because the firm was interested in starting a plant tissue cloning business in Casper.

I'm constantly studying. Being in this business has taught me that people really want information along with their purchase; they want the right answers, and they expect you to have them. There are so many facets of this business that are interesting and far-reaching, from plant propagation and fertilization, to heating and cooling, and finding out what our return is on x number of plants for this many weeks on so much bench space.

Right now I feel like the shoemaker's child; the biggest liability of being in the nursery business is that I don't have time for my own garden. But often there's a lot of satisfaction at the end of the day. Last night when I came home, I went out to make sure the willows were watered, and it's like making nursing rounds; I go in and say good night, and that's it for the day.

My biggest frustration is being unable to call someone back and reassure them about a tree or plant problem. Summer days are very long ones, and I'm often not home until nine at night because I'm making yard calls. I feel very responsible for the rapport between the customer and our place, and I like everybody to be very satisfied with our services. Sometimes we fail because everybody wants to think they are our only customer, but we want them to feel that way too!

So we do a lot of hand-holding in this business. We had a very bad season when people lost many big trees. People actually went through the grief and grieving process. You could see it. They'd come out and say, "You know Hazel, that great big tree in our backyard that's not doing too well, why it had to be two, three feet around." They were grieving, and they weren't yet ready to replace "her," as they'd refer to that tree. And I'd say, "That's okay, watch it a couple of weeks." And pretty soon they'd come back and say, "There's just no hope, she's gone. We've got to do something." And pretty soon they'd get started on it. It has taught me that people, for the most part, feel about their yards like they do about their family. Most of all I enjoy working with people, with their personal and psychological needs for their yards and trees.

Dr. Derald Langham in his garden in the Mohawk Valley.

Derald Langham
GARDENING IN CIRCLES

In 1972, the President of Venezuela decorated Dr. Derald Langham with the Order of Merit of Performance, the highest honor ever given a foreigner by the Venezuelan government. The award was an acknowledgment of Derald's development of many different crops for Venezuela thirty years earlier. He is one of the world's foremost experts in corn and sesame, and also a tireless educator. Now in his seventies, Derald lives in Wellton, Arizona, and continues to work with sesame, to share the method he has developed of gardening in circles, and to teach people how to develop their full potential.

141

I was born on a 160-acre farm in Iowa. I had everything a child could want: a nice family, a nice home, hills, valleys, big trees, fields, and waving grass to play in. From the time we were really young, my two brothers and sister and I were milking the cows, feeding the calves and hogs, and driving the horses; we learned how to do everything on the farm. When I was ten years old, I was driving five horses on a big old plow, with three behind and two horses way out front, and cultivating the field with a team of horses, and dragging—all the farm operations.

The part I remember most vividly was the springtime. I would roll out of bed just before daybreak, mount my horse bareback, and go riding over the hills through the pastures to see which particular mares had had colts during the night, which particular ewes had lambed, which particular cows had calved, and which sows had had pigs and how many. Then I would return to the farm to see how many ducklings were hatched during the night, how many baby chicks, how many goslings, and so on.

I also loved to plant things and watch them come up. I wanted to be a farmer, but to deal with animals primarily. I didn't necessarily want to be a veterinarian; I wanted to be more like a herdsman, because I related so much to the animals.

As a boy, I discovered when I went into the woods and stood or sat by a very large tree, if I was absolutely quiet, the squirrels, groundhogs, and rabbits would forget I was there. I found that if I got quiet that way and closed my eyes, I could sense everything without seeing it, even to know if there were birds flying overhead.

In high school, I had an agricultural teacher who always said, "If anybody should go to college, you should be the one, Derald." So I went to Iowa State College to study agronomy. My very first quarter there I had an interesting professor, a big rough and tough guy, who one day asked to see me after class. I was really scared, but all he said was "What do you know about genetics?" I said, "I don't know what it is. I can't even spell it." He said, "Well, you see resemblances and differences. You notice how things are alike and how they are different. And that's the main qualification of a geneticist. So if you want, I'll take you over to the head of the Department of Genetics, Dr. Lindstrom, and introduce you."

Dr. Lindstrom was even more rough and gruff, a big old Swede. He didn't want to talk very much; he just handed me a cloth bag full of corn seeds, all different colors, sizes, shapes, sugaries, flints, and everything else, and asked me to classify them. I took them into the laboratory and sorted them according to what they were, and made a list of how many seeds there were and each kind. There were thousands of them. I went back to the other room, and he said in his very gruff way, "What are you doing back here? You couldn't have sorted them out that quickly." He went in, looked at what I had done, and said, "When do you want to go to work? We need to get you ready to be a geneticist."

The two of them worked out my schedule for the next four years. I had to take statistics, mathematics, German, French, and the hard sciences. What made it so difficult was that often two or three of my required classes were offered at the same time. Since I couldn't be in three places at once, I spent a lot of my time skipping one class to go to another. That was a job, but I did it. Then Dr. Lindstrom sent me to R. A. Emerson, the top plant geneticist at the time at Cornell, and I got my doctorate there.

In 1939, I was hired to be the geneticist at the first agricultural experiment station in Venezuela. My wife and I planned to be there only a year or two. I started to work on corn, my specialty, and then on some of the other crops. I made a trip around the country and found that there were plenty of starches—roots and tubers and all kinds of things—but the people were starving for fats and proteins. I looked at soybeans and peanuts and sunflowers and all the usual, and ran into sesame. About 50 percent of its weight is oil and 26 percent is protein. It has a very good balance of minerals and is rich in vitamins, especially the B group. You can eat very well by building your diet around sesame and adding whatever you want. So I began to work with that, too.

I had made all the crosses when the Second World War broke out. At that time, Venezuela was importing a good deal of its food, and when German submarines began to harass Caribbean shipping lanes, the plant improvement and development project turned into a crash program to make the country agriculturally self-sufficient. Suddenly there wasn't time to follow standard procedures for sorting all the crosses out.

I went back to what I did as a boy. I would walk down to the fields before sunrise and empty myself of any knowledge of the plants that I had. That took some doing. Then I'd walk into a field of five thousand segregated populations of sesame and say, "I need to know which ones of you have the highest oil, and which ones will yield the best, and which ones will the farmer really want," and so on. And wherever I was stopped in the field by the sesame itself, I

A large circle garden under construction; the raised and fenced circumference is designed to keep lizards out.

would just collect seed. It worked beautifully for rice, beans, sorghum, and potatoes as well.

It still does. At seventy-six I'm still doing it, my whole family does it, and anyone who wants to learn it can. That is part of what we do in the program I've started called Genesa, which is all about developing human potential into a functional reality, because the energy field which envelops the plants is very similar to the energy field which envelops people.

I wasn't talking to the plants, I was communicating with them. Plants don't have brains, but they do have minds, so it was mind-to-mind communication. I was using what I call The Four I's: Instinct, Intuition, Insight, and Inspiration, which all work from the spirit center of each person. These work with a very fine type of energies, what I now call the superenergies.

The instincts work with the life force; the intuitions with the love force; the insights with the light force; and the inspiration with the let force, the willingness to let go and let God. I empty myself of all thought of my own body and of the structure of the plant, and let go.

I relax into the mind of the sesame itself, then work through the instinct and intuition and insight, and ask what I need to know. Normally I get individual words, but when there is really good contact between my biofield and the biofield of the plant, I get whole paragraphs, and can translate from the energies I sense into words.

I didn't talk about what I was doing with anyone because I knew I would be discredited if I did. I just kept working for the Venezuelan government. They put me in charge of agriculture for the whole country. When the war was over, I settled down to just the Department of Genetics and Agronomy, with sixty people on my staff and about two hundred fifty field men. Then the Communists moved in, took over the country, and kicked all the Americans out of their jobs in the government. I was the last to leave because the farmers didn't want me to go.

I had worked for the government for ten years, and I stayed in Venezuela for ten more, setting up my own seed, landscape, and nursery company. I ended up with five hundred men on my payroll and six big nurseries in different parts of the country. We landscaped twenty small cities for oil companies, putting in all their parks and landscaping around their hospitals, schools, administration buildings, streets, and everything else.

I had also set up a nursery on my own property, because the government had allowed me to keep my own plant material. I had thousands of varieties of sesame and tried to plant them in straight rows. But the land was a little sloping; when we had heavy rains, sheet erosion would take place. The seeds were light—50 percent oil—and had a tendency to rise in the soil anyway, so they would be carried away along with the water.

To prevent that, I disked up all my fields and created sets of one hundred circles each. I would drive ten stakes into the ground at regular intervals and pull the soil away from those stakes into circles. Then I would stand in each circle and pull the soil toward the ridge. I made ten rows with ten circles each; it ended up looking like a bunch of hula-hoop-sized tires made of soil in the field, with a little basin in the center of each one. I would plant one family halfway down the inner slope of the circle and not worry about the rain. The seeds didn't float away because there wasn't enough water in the center to create sheet erosion. Using that kind of grid, it was easy to keep the families separate and to know what was growing where.

What we weren't prepared to find was that the sesame grew better in circles than they did in straight rows, so much so that the farmers came around and asked, "Why don't mine grow like that? Your plants look a lot better than mine." I realized it was because the circle supported a plant's natural spiral pattern of growth. Growth occurs actually in three main ways: as a pulse, a creative force; as a wave, a formative force; and as a spiral, a functional force.

Another way to put it is that growth is energy moving in spirals through living plants at varying rates of spin. Look at a little pea plant—or anything that climbs—spiral around. If you looked right down on the plant with a slow camera, you would see the whole plant spiral. The Fibonacci series, the way the leaves are positioned, is related to the spiral also.

So when you put a dozen plants around in a circle, then each plant has its own spiral, but together they make a family spiral. If you put, as I have in my garden here, six more circles around that one, you get a bigger spiral. And if you take that and put six more sets of seven around it, you get a tremendous vortex of energy. As we know from cyclones and our weather systems, the power is in the vortex.

Circle gardening has many advantages besides working in harmony with the natural growth pattern of plants. The basin

Seedlings, planted halfway down the inside rim, are protected from the wind and have easy access to the water and composting materials in the center.

around which the plants grow, the hollow of the circle, is slightly lower than the natural soil level and seems to permit a penetration into the energy field of the earth. Even a slight breeze blowing across the ridge of the circle sets up a vortex of energy that "feeds" the plants.

Only the inner side of the circle is watered, thereby conserving water. The outside of the circle remains dry, allowing for a vital interchange of gases with the soil. Soil additives, compost and such, are placed only inside the circle, giving maximum results. The spacing permits good air movement and good penetration of sunlight among the plants. The interspersing of different types of plants reduces disease and insect damage. Where it does occur, it is easier to control.

Circles are convenient for the gardener to move about in, to plant or cross or harvest or maneuver a wheelbarrow or keep track of how each plant is doing. The amount of physical work is reduced once the circles have been set up because you only work the inner surface of each ridge. The circles I use have an inner diameter of one meter and inner circumference of ten feet. That's the equivalent of a ten-foot row, so it is easy to calculate and apply chemical fertilizer, if you use that. I no longer do; I only use manure.

Circles also favor the microorganisms. At New York State University, they have proven that the levels of phosphorous, nitrogen, and potassium are increased inside the circles without adding fertilizer to the soil itself. The increase in flora and fauna of the soil such as actinomycetes, bacteria, fungi, earthworms, and so on, releases elements from the earth itself. This is true of circles planted with anything, but especially sesame.

Gardening in circles reminds us of how we are connected to the earth. Physicists tell us that on the molecular level there is no difference between "organic" and "inorganic" life. The earth is a living organism, and we need to treat it like a living organism. It involves everything in the earth itself, including all the waters and soils and rocks, and extends beyond the surface of the earth into the atmosphere. All these peace movements and environmental groups that are going on right now are an outcry of people who are realizing we've got to do something about protecting Mother Earth.

That is one of the reasons we are doing intensive work to create new lines of sesame. It has the highest biofield of any plant that I know. My son-in-law calls sesame plants "fountains of living energy." We know that sesame brings cosmic energy into the soil, and recharges it. If you walk in a sesame field or eat it or just carry the pods around in your pocket, you get recharged. You just feel different in a sesame field, vibrant, alive. Your mind is sharp and everything works. One of our grandchildren's favorite things is to take a picnic lunch on Sundays into the sesame fields, and the sesame likes kids, too.

We are, of course, looking for other uses of sesame beyond food, and to extend its use as a food. In Venezuela, the first thing we made was a sesame milkshake. When enough sesame appears in this country, they'll start offering that here, too. People will want sesame ice cream and sesame health drinks, and to mix sesame with other high energy foods to make superenergy foods.

Anyway, our big thrust is to get enough sesame around the earth to help recharge and restore the whole earth. Right now we're working in an area of Texas where sugar beet farming has depleted the soil. We're farming thousands of acres using traditional row methods because the farmers we are working with are geared to that.

It would be difficult to farm on a large scale using circles because there is no machinery. However, when they first started large-scale farming in straight rows, there wasn't any machinery to deal with that either; the machinery was developed because the method was already there. If people really went to work on growing in circles on a large scale, someone would invent the machinery to do it.

Sesame can quickly revitalize an area. We've created, with sesame's help, plants which, when they get physiologically ripe, shed their leaves, improving the flora and fauna of the soil. The actinomycetes and bacteria and fungi counts build up very fast. In addition, the sesame plants release chemicals that are tied up in the soil. This is a natural process that is favored by greater counts of microorganisms.

Basically what we've been able to do with The Four I's, as I call it, is to help sesame develop its own potential. We're trying to get our mind in agreement with the sesame in the presence of God, and then figure out what we want. If the sesame can do it without violating any of its principles or natural principles, then it will juggle its genes to do it. That's the whole big breakthrough. It is the relationship between the mind of the plant breeder, the mind of the plant or animal, and a third party, God, always has to be there, too.

The genes are not changed, but they're juggled. Most of our genes are asleep; they don't even wake up during our whole lifetime. A sesame can, by its own mind, wake up the genes that it needs to wake up, and make gene teams to do specific things. Just as with a piano's set of keys, anyone can go plunkety plunk, but a real pianist can sit down and draw out some of the potential of the piano. The piano is still the same as it was, the keys have not been changed. The so-called big mystery of genetics, of what turns the genes on and off, is no mystery at all to me. It's your mind.

From my work in Venezuela, sesame spread up through Central America, but it didn't become a crop in the United States because a lot of hand labor was involved. You could grow it and cut it with a grain binder, but then the bundles all fell on the ground. You had to have people set the bundles into shocks, wait until they got ripe, and then throw them into a combine.

So what we have created with the help of sesame is a sesame pod that just barely opens a little at the tip. Now, when the pod is physiologically ripe and the stalk drops its leaves, we go through with a swather, make a wind row, and let the stalks dry in the sun. Then we come through with a combine with a pickup attachment and pick them right up, so there is no hand labor involved.

I make it sound easy but this has involved many years of work on the part of many people. We had a lot of problems with diseases and such, and finally one day in the early eighties in one of my communications with sesame, it finally just said to me in an outright way, "We refuse. We want to be a crop but we don't want to be a slave to man. If you close our pod up completely, it will require man to open it if we are to propagate ourselves. If man disappears and we are left with that, we can't propagate."

Everything man has domesticated he has made a slave out of, like the ear of corn. The wild type has loose seeds that just scatter. Then when a type came along with a solid ear, man selected that because it was easier to harvest. If a solid ear drops to the soil, it will not propagate itself because so many of the kernels germinate that they choke themselves to death. They depend on man to scatter them.

Another good example is the difference between range cows and milk cows. The range cow only gives enough milk for her calf. But man wanted milk for himself, so he developed these Holsteins, Jerseys, and Guernseys with lots of milk. If they were left out on the range without anyone to milk them, the calf can't take all the milk and the cow develops milk fever and dies. These cows have become slaves to man.

The sesame is naturally a wild plant and doesn't want to be dominated. After many years of work we were able to create this pod which opens just a little at the top, so that 5 percent of the seed can get out and propagate itself if man is not around. It has other advantages because, when the pod gets nearly ripe, if it is closed, the moisture inside can't get out. With this open tip the pods dry faster and also thresh a lot easier in the combine. The sesame is playing its own piano to create these kinds of pods, and we're propagating them and intercrossing them and compounding the genes and so forth. So now it's better for us, and it is better for the sesame.

Another thing I've developed is the concept of the flexible middle, of crossing the best and the worst. When I was in Venezuela and had all the students helping me in the big crash plant-breeding program, I taught them how to make crosses in sesame. Usually we had a scheduled program, but sometimes they'd come back in the middle of the afternoon and say, "What do I cross now?" and I'd occasionally say, "Well, cross anything you want."

My system was to act like the head of the department during the day, but early in the morning before daybreak and late in the afternoon after everyone went home, I would go out into the fields until dark and relax into the sesame. One night, in about 1943, I noticed a plant with more glands on its leaves than I had ever seen. I checked it out, and found it was a cross a student had made; the plant with the most glands crossed with the plant with the least. I started checking that out and found that consistently where I crossed the most glands with the least glands, I got the supergland types. So I said, "If that is the way nature works, let's work with it," and started extending the idea.

I crossed plants that were completely destroyed by aphids with plants which were semiresistant. You get types that are even more susceptible, but more important, you get plants that are nearly immune. You can pick those and they will breed true. It's called transgressive segregation, but it's supertransgressive because I cross it with the other end. I got so excited that I came up to the United States and lectured at Harvard, Yale, Cornell, Iowa State, and Ohio State. I showed them the results in pictures, but nobody picked up on it. It just didn't make sense to them. Anyway, I published in *Science* and *Journal of Crop Sciences*, so it's there for people when they want it.

This concept of the flexible middle, of crossing the best with the worst for a better one, worked very well with corn, too, and I developed a plant that increased the yield of corn in Venezuela by 400

Derald and eight of his grandchildren playing in a large circle garden. Each of the seven circles has been named after one of his four children and three foster children; he likes to think about each person as he gardens in that circle. The geometric structures are used as learning tools in his Genesa program, portions of which have recently been adopted by a number of Montessori schools in Texas.

percent. That corn was so strong that it could adapt to almost any kind of climate. It started to be used in Central America and Colombia and Brazil and all those places, but it began to wipe out all the local strains that had been there for probably thousands of years, all that wonderful germ plasm. So a corn seed bank was set up to save the native strains.

When I came back from Venezuela in 1958, I realized that with this concept of the flexible middle, I'd been able to help the plants develop their best potential, their best selves, and it ought to be possible to do that with people, too. So I went back to school to get my second Ph.D. to learn about epistemology and axiology and ontology to set up a system to teach people how to activate their own potential, and specifically how to activate their genes at will and build gene teams. I needed to learn the jargon so that I could talk with the educators, the philosophers, psychologists, and so on, to share the program I now call Genesa. I've spent most of my time developing this and working with sesame, but I still garden here as I've done all my life. I love to get out there and work early in the morning when everyone is still asleep. Circle gardening is a way to focus on the plants, the soil, and people, all intermingled together as one. It's a therapy, if you like.

Countries can also be fighting politically, but the agriculturists will exchange information without worrying about politics. Developing new garden techniques and working in agriculture have been ways for me to cut across political borders, ways to help create world family harmony by developing plant and human potentials.

I don't use the word *peace* because, for many people, peace simply means absence of conflict. Harmony is different; it is a dynamic equilibrium. Its main ingredients are balance, rhythm, and symmetry. It's give and take. Basically it is genetics again, figuring out how we're alike and how we're different and finding a way to combine them to have the best of both.

The Garden as Healer

Catherine Sneed Marcum holding an herb; the prisoners have an extensive herb garden as well as a vegetable garden.

Catherine Sneed Marcum
GARDENING BEHIND BARS

Gardening has helped many of us through difficult times: the death of someone dear, the pain of a divorce, or of children leaving the nest. Catherine Sneed Marcum, however, credits gardening with saving her life. Suffering from a life-threatening illness for which the medical world offered no hope, she decided to see if working with the soil could help both herself and the prisoners she counseled at the San Francisco County Jail. In the process not only did Catherine experience a remission of her own disease, she also created a unique jail horticultural program that combines job training with counseling, offering prisoners both literally and metaphorically the chance for "a new start."

*I*n 1982, I was very ill with a serious kidney disease. That, coupled with my very stressful counseling job at the San Francisco County Jail and my family responsibilities, was almost too much. I was really going down.

My doctor said, "The chemotherapy isn't working. I don't know what to do. You could stay in the hospital or you could go home." I went home, and I came to work the next day. I could barely walk, and I looked very funny because I had edema, which is severe water retention. As a woman, it was very hard to walk around looking funny. But I got past it, and I think I got past it by gardening.

I've been in remission now for several years. My doctor is a nice person who now feels that the chemotherapy did it. I don't feel that. I feel gardening and the changes I made in my diet put me in remission, and saved my life.

Gardening has given me personal strength, and focused me. I feel I'm a brand new person that I didn't dream I could be. My attitude has changed; I have hope that my life's work, counseling, means something.

I started as a camp counselor in high school and did that for about six years. Then I wanted to be a lawyer. I went to law school, and learned that lawyers don't get a chance to counsel. That's not their job, even though they're called "counselors." So, around 1981, I began working at the San Francisco County Jail as a counselor.

But I found that I was not getting the prisoners' attention. They were not focusing on what we were talking about because they were in tremendous pain, and because jail is such a crazy, chaotic place, with very painful things happening all around. It also became clear to me that even if we were able to get down to why they were here, and what they wanted to do with their lives, there was still a serious block. They didn't have basic educational or job skills to make different lives for themselves.

When I was a kid, my father had an incredible rose garden. We had a lot of kids in our family, and we'd always work every weekend, slaving away in his rose garden. But I always thought I couldn't grow anything. I never had a house plant that lived, for instance. What made me become interested in gardening was reading Steinbeck's *The Grapes of Wrath* when I was in the hospital and very sick. I was really inspired by how those people drew strength from the soil.

I realized that the people I was working with were like the people in *The Grapes of Wrath*. They're independent, these men and women, and think they are going to make it on their own. The problem is that they are making it in a socially unacceptable way, through criminal activity, so they don't really make it at all. I thought that if they had a legal way of making it, perhaps they would take that way. I felt that if gardening could heal me, with a physical illness, then it could heal these people with emotional illnesses. So that is what inspired me to become a gardener—the combination of being sick, and of feeling like I was getting nowhere with the people I was counseling. Not because they didn't like me or because I didn't have rapport with them, but because they had no way to make it in the world.

There were wonderful buildings and equipment on the jail grounds left over from when the county jail had operated a farm to grow all its own food. I thought it was a shame to waste this space and the prisoners' time. There is nothing to do here. We literally have a captive audience. Many of them can spend their whole jail sentences, which can be up to a year, watching television, playing cards, fighting—all out of pure boredom. The median age here is twenty-four. A lot of them begin at eighteen, going nowhere. I thought gardening would be an alternative for them and for myself, as well.

I started this program in 1984. Some of the prisoners and I cleaned up and fixed the old greenhouses that were just rotting away. Then we started a small market garden. Some of the produce was used here at the jail; some was sold to a few local restaurants and to two of the largest local organic food stores in San Francisco. My biggest problem was that I could not always supply the demand. One of the stores wanted us to come every other day with an incredible volume. But because this is a jail, there would be an emergency or a jail suicide, and they'd lock down the jail, so we couldn't work in the garden or get the produce out.

Every evening, after my husband and I got our kids in bed, I would start reading, trying to figure out what to do. It was driving me nuts, not having a real horticultural background. I knew that this program really had a potential to grow, and it needed someone who really knew what they were doing. So I decided to take a leave from my counseling position and go to school. I did the first semester at Emerson College in England, studying biodynamic gardening. But I found their course more designed for farmers than for gardeners, and I missed my family terribly. So I came back, apprenticed at the

Catherine in the San Francisco County Jail greenhouse which she and the inmates restored.

Green Gulch Farm in Marin, and then did the agro-ecology program at the University of California at Santa Cruz.

There are about seven hundred men and about fifty women at the jail, and I counsel both populations. I get constant requests from prisoners wanting to join this program, but only a small percentage are able to participate. Some see it as a possibility for employment, and some just see it as a chance to grow things, or to be outside, where it is serene and quiet.

They also know that it is a small group, and they will be treated like a person. I really respect them. I deal with them as I would deal with anyone, and as I would want someone to deal with me or my family. I ask them to give 100 percent—all that they have. I ask everyone in the class to work as hard as they can, and to be respectful of people who maybe aren't respectful of them. I ask, but I also demand. I don't accept less. I think that is understood by the rest of the jail population.

I ask that they understand that we're a team. We're working together. And what we're doing is more important than ourselves. I tell them to accept the benefit of that. When I first say it, these guys laugh and say, "Ha! ha! She's so funny." But then they see that I mean it. The prisoners see how much gardening has meant to me.

I use gardening as a metaphor. When we're double-digging and preparing a bed, I can say, "You know what we're doing? Sure, we're preparing this seedbed and it is hard work, but also we're preparing a home; just like you need your home to be safe, to have the things that help you to grow, so do these plants." So I'm constantly able to use metaphors that apply to their own lives.

Because it is an organic garden, I am able to say, "Well, we could take this chemical here and spray it on this stuff. But what's it going to do to us? What's it going to do to the other plants? It's just like you. When you shoot up heroin, what does it do to you? What does it do to your family? What does it do to society? It's the same thing." It's the clearest way I've found to help them think about what's happening in their lives. I think it changes the way they see the world, or it can.

It certainly doesn't do it for everyone, but some see the similarity. No one has nurtured these guys, and they haven't seen a lot of nurturing around them. They're learning to nurture something in the garden and they're being nurtured by this something. I say that all the time. You know, I've had these big bad tough guys say to me, "Oh Cathy, this is girls' work. I don't want to do nothin' with these plants." And two weeks later the same macho giant with the tattoos and the tracks down his arm is out there saying, "Hey, don't step on my babies!"

So there is a possibility that I, along with the plants, can give these people some hope to go on with their lives, or even to make a life, because that isn't happening in their lives now, or in the prison system. There is no hope here, there is no life; it is all death and scars and pain.

None of these people are here for life; most of them are going to go back where they came from. So I think it makes sense to try to give people hope; otherwise they come back with rage and pain and take it out on everyone else. Prisons have operated jail farms forever, but I don't think there are any programs doing horticulture as therapy, which is what we're doing. But it's not just therapy: it's job training and counseling as well.

It reminds me of when I was a camp counselor, where you nurture the inner city children for a short period of time and then they go back to an unnurturing world. But still, it's like a seed. It's planted somewhere, and you never know, maybe the conditions will happen to make it grow. And maybe not.

I think gardening has the potential to make people whole again, and unless people are whole, they're not going to make it. They're not going to stay out of jail, and they're not going to stop doing bad things to other people. A lot of people here do bad things to other people because they had bad things done to them and because they don't see a connection between themselves and society. I think gardening shows the connection. They see how the plants are connected to the earth and how we are connected to the plants. That's how the becoming whole happens, or can happen.

In the beginning, when I tried to start this program, everybody thought I was nuts. First of all, the staff didn't think that I would get the prisoners involved, or that they would be interested. And even if they were mildly interested, the staff thought that I could not get them to work because they were lazy good-for-nothings who were afraid of work, basically bad people.

My experience is that the prisoners outwork anybody that I've ever seen. Now the staff sees that the prisoners want to come outside and work, even in the pouring rain. They come in muddy and excited, talking about the work and saying things like, "Well, I'm going to get a job." The staff saw prisoners get jobs, and it is slowly changing their attitudes.

The prisoners don't get a dime. They do it because they know that they're learning, they like what they are doing, and the money made from the program goes back to the City of San Francisco. I think this is also part of the healing process. The prisoners have done something bad to society and to themselves. In order to be healed, they have to feel that they are able to give something back.

The prisoners have also involved the other staff. They started explaining to the deputies and others what they were doing out there. They gave them our leftover seedlings, explaining how to care for the plants. Now there are some deputies and staff who have started gardens, and I see the difference in them, too. They come in with, "This is happening in my garden. . . ."

It's also made a difference for me. I'm a civilian here, a woman, and I'm black. All those things got together and it was hard for the other staff to even think of me as a person. Gardening has brought us together as nothing else did.

There is a bad attitude in this culture about work, physical work. That's another thing that I try to teach the prisoners with gardening. It's your attitude that counts. If you see it as demeaning, then it is demeaning. A lot of these guys say, "No, I'm not going to do any physical labor, or pick up a shovel. I want to be a pimp." Where does that attitude come from? Some of it comes from society saying when you do physical labor, you're like a slave. One way to get these guys to rethink that is to see me doing physical labor. They see that it doesn't make me less of a person.

Also, I constantly talk about what important work we're doing. I remind them that the person double-digging the beds is as important as the person that drives the tractor. They see how compost is the most important thing that we deal with—it's not garbage.

Catherine's garden at home, which both she and her husband enjoy tending.

We have to change that attitude for our youngsters as well. One of my daughters once said to me, "Mom, I want to be like you when I grow up, but I don't want to be a gardener!" What she was saying was, "I don't want to be dirty all the time. You're always covered with something, and the mommies on TV aren't covered with something; they're always clean and they don't have manure under their fingernails or muddy boots. . . ."

And I said, "You can be like me when you grow up, and you know that I am a gardener." I want my daughters to see me doing something I want to do, something that I choose to do, something I'm learning because I want to learn it, and that I've had to sacrifice to do.

This program really does excite me, but it's hard because it's in a jail, with all the despair, horror, and pain of that. But I like what I'm doing and I like the people I work with. I feel that I'm doing something to help society and myself. It is important to me that these people get healed, because I want them to have that opportunity for themselves, and because I have children. I want them to live in a healed world.

John Tuttle in a cap that reflects his love of birds.

John Tuttle
FINDING PATIENCE AND PEACE

John Tuttle moved from Texas to Billings, Montana, just as the Depression started. He fell in love with the wilderness and the mountains and never returned to his home state. Gardening in Montana, however, is not easy; the average number of growing days is 134. Yet in spite of the short season, he and his wife have been finding ways to grow vegetables and ornamentals for over fifty years. Gardening gives John far more than flowers or food for his table; it offers a feast for his eyes and his camera, a way to share the beauties of nature with the young and old, and peace for his soul.

I'm interested in anything that grows. I go to the mountains and I look at trees a lot. When I see a tree that grows in a twist, I think what agonies that tree must go through, growing twisted up like that. The way to get acquainted with a tree is to work in a one-horse sawmill, where you can cut the tree, haul it to the mill, and run it through the saws yourself. You see the stress as the slabs come off, and you'd be surprised at the stress that grows in a tree. In one sense, you can kind of read its life. When you stop to think about it, the wind and sun and gravity and moisture are all working on that tree. Gravity is trying to pull it to the ground, the sun is trying to pull it in the air, and it's fighting the wind. It makes you realize that life is difficult even for a tree. Even a tree doesn't have things its own way.

When I was a kid at home, we used to have to work in the garden. It wasn't fun then. Anything anybody told me to do, why, I didn't want to do it. And if they told me not to do it, why then I'd break my neck to do it. I'm pretty obstinate. My sister's husband always said, "If there's anything more stubborn than a Missouri mule, it's a Tuttle."

But since I got on my own, gardening has been fun. It's a relaxation. I worked in the carpentry trade for many years, for a commercial outfit, and on many of the jobs I was the foreman. Things would come up that I'd just get frustrated over. I'd come home and grab a hoe and chop heck out of the garden when it didn't even need it. It was a way of working off tension, because you can build up a lot of tension in the city, especially if you're inclined to be a country hick.

I love the beauty of the mountains here. I like to go into them to hike or to just be alone, wandering around with my camera. If I get a picture, it is a bonus; I enjoy being there regardless. I don't have any patience to fish, so I'm not a fisherman. But I can sit and wait for hours for the wind to stop blowing so I can take a picture of a wildflower or the various shades of greens or something like that. You know, when God made all that stuff, he didn't intend for colors to clash, and they don't.

I like to stop and study the flowers. I keep a little hand magnifying lens with me most of the time that I can put right down in the flower and really see what's there. I like photography a lot too, and it's kind of a toss-up which one, gardening or photography, has got priority. I think they go hand in hand.

Before I retired a few years ago due to my arthritis, I was up before daylight lots of mornings to put in a shift in the garden before

Beans and cabbage thrive despite the short Montana summer; not an inch in John's garden is wasted.

I went to work, and it was the same way when I came home in the evening. I like whatever chores come up in the garden. I enjoy planting a seed and watching it grow. To me it's a miracle that we just don't think about.

I get to looking at the plants, and if they don't do right I wonder what to do with them. I'll dope one with this and one with that, and forget which one I doped with what. Sometimes it will come out of it and sometimes it gives up, so I don't know any more really than I did before. In fact, when it comes to nature and plant life and things of that kind, I think the older I get the dumber I get. The more I know, the more I see what I don't know. There are so many things to know, and you can't know it all.

A lot of people think that if you're a good gardener you shouldn't have any weeds in your garden, but I think they're wrong. A certain percentage of weeds in a garden gives your plants nutrients that they don't get anywhere else. Take the redrooted pigweed, for example. It grows way down deep and brings up minerals that vegetables don't have, minerals that they need to grow and can't get anywhere else.

I think the secret of good gardening is compost. When my wife and I first moved to this house in 1959, this area was an old alkali swamp. Long about July, if you wanted to hoe the garden, you had to get a pickax to do it. I've had to build up the garden everywhere. Some of it has probably been built up about fourteen inches with compost, with no garden soil in it. I hauled in leaves from all over the city, along with sawdust from the mills and grass clippings. No doubt I've got a few pesticides from other people's gardens that shouldn't be there, but it still grows pretty good tomatoes.

But I'm just coming to the conclusion that there's something that I can't put there. There's something lacking in it, minerals and stuff in soil that I can't put in the garden. Man can't make soil. He can improve the soil, but he can't make it. And that's just what I've been trying to do here for all these years. They say that it takes anywhere from five hundred to a thousand years to make an inch of good topsoil, so I guess I shouldn't have expected to do it in thirty.

I grow just about everything from seed. That's the fun of gardening! I have put a glass greenhouse on the end of my garage. I start the greenhouse up about the middle of December. Sometimes, if I can get it, I'll have the pansy seed in by November. In the winter I make a big compost pile next to the greenhouse and put pipe in it which brings the heat from the compost pile into the greenhouse. It has kind of an odor in there all right, but the plants don't mind it a bit, and so I don't mind it, either.

My wife and I both garden, but we split it up. She has the front end of the yard and I have the back end. That way we keep from duplicating things and getting in each other's way. In the wintertime when it's too cold to garden, we get a couple dozen catalogs and comb through those.

But gardening in this area is not easy. It's too cold in the spring and stays too cold, but then I like all the seasons and wouldn't want to live someplace where the seasons didn't change. I get a little disgusted with the late snows, but then, so what? You can't do

The Tuttles' cozy backyard: the area close to the house is filled with ornamentals, while the vegetable garden is largely out of view.

anything about it. I think as far as I'm concerned, this area has got everything I want.

I'm an outdoors person, and I like to be alone a lot. I like people, but I don't like big bunches of them. I get frustrated when there are too many people around. I think everybody should, sometime in his life, learn to be by himself. One nice thing about gardening is that it's something you can do by yourself. And yet I never really feel alone. Christ is riding right on my shoulder all the time.

And then, too, when you read through Genesis in the Bible, it tells you to take care of the soil, to put back into it what you take out of it, and about all the insect infestations that will always be there. Last year the whole western half of Montana had a bad infestation of grasshoppers. One morning we got up and there were grasshoppers everywhere. I told my wife when we went in to eat breakfast that it looked like they would eat us up. That same day the birds moved in—grackles and starlings and sparrows and finches—and they worked this block. These lawns were just about black with the birds, and when they were done, you hardly saw a grasshopper.

When we moved in here, you'd be surprised how many different kinds of insects there were. A long time ago we sprayed quite a bit, and finally we quit because I could see we weren't getting anywhere. I started feeding the birds. I figured if I could feed them in the morning when they first get up, and if each bird eats two or three worms out of this garden before they leave to go somewhere else, well, that's going to cut down a lot of worms. We probably spend a couple of hundred dollars a year for bird seed, but it's well worth it.

Birds are just like sheep. When you first look at them they all look alike, but when you herd them a little bit, they turn out to be individuals, like people. I built the fountain in our yard for the birds out of a whole menagerie of different kinds of brick and stone. It turned out pretty well; the birds took right to it.

One of the nicest sights I think anybody could ever see is when the yellow warblers bring their young in here to the fountain for the first time. One end of it is real shallow, and those little birds love to get in there and get their feet wet. It's a beautiful sight, and worth all the effort I put into it.

I like to work with wood, to build things, and to work with my hands. I got mixed up with the Bluebird Society of America and volunteered to build birdhouses for them if they furnished the lumber. I've built two hundred of them now in the past two years.

I'd say all my hobbies involve nature: gardening, hiking, bird watching, and photography. I take my slides of birds and flowers and put on slide shows for the Billings Camera Club, nursing homes, and for the children in the schools. Then I feel like I've accomplished something. If you can go into a school with twenty-five or thirty kids in kindergarten and first, second, and third grades, and keep them quiet for twenty or twenty-five minutes, you've done pretty well.

I suppose gardening has taught me patience, and through patience you get tranquillity. And through both of those, you get a real nice feeling of being at peace with the world. I don't try to change nature. I think the good Lord's done a good job, and I don't think I could improve on it.

Wendy Johnson tending the roses at Green Gulch Farm.

Wendy Johnson
BRINGING GARDENS TO THE WORLD

Webster's Dictionary defines a nursery as "a room or place appropriate to the care of children; a place for training and education; a place where trees, shrubs, and vines are propagated for transplanting." During a visit to the nurseries of the Zen Center's Green Gulch Farm outside of Sausalito, California, I realized that there all three meanings applied. There was a safe, well-cared-for atmosphere, and looking at flat after flat of seedlings, I had the sense almost of little children having been tucked cozily into bed. Attention was paid to every detail of the gardening process, including bringing the water for seedlings to room temperature before it was applied. Such careful attention reflects not only the Zen philosophy on which the farm is based, but also the horticultural orientation of its head gardener, Wendy Johnson.

The house where I grew up in Westport, Connecticut, had a screened porch. When we were little, we would look out over the May-flowering viburnum and watch the fireflies. By the time I was in high school, these same shrubs enclosed the porch, and I started sleeping in this porch room. It was like living inside the core of a fragrant viburnum forest. I think a lot of my love for gardening originated from growing up in that beautiful place and helping to take care of it over the years.

My parents bought the house right after the war. It was a very beautiful big old house, but falling apart a little when my parents got it. The people who lived there before had obviously given all their attention to the gardens. There was a magnificent magnolia and huge old maples and lots of roses storming over the garden walls. They had established gorgeous gardens rather on the order of the White Flower Farm in Litchfield, Connecticut.

It was a kind of rambly old place, with big fragrant lilacs and rhododendrons to hide under—a very woodsy place. My mother loved to be in the garden; she would be outside puttering around whenever she could. It was where we lived and played all summer. The garden was home.

It was also a refuge, the one thing that was steady in a rather chaotic world. My parents had a rough marriage and finally did separate. Although my love for my family was also very steady, our emotional situation was rugged. So I remember spending hours in the garden. It was a real relief.

I grew up and lived in that one house until I went away to college. I'm sure that made a big difference in my life. And because of living on the East Coast, I had a real sense and appreciation for the changing seasons, and the whole rhythm of nature intertwined with our lives.

I've always been a rural person and have always been somehow connected to gardening, either by just being in the natural world, or actually taking care of gardens. I've never lived in a city, except for one year in Israel when I studied classical Hebrew in Jerusalem. For the last twelve years I've lived here at Green Gulch Farm, in Marin County, seventeen miles from metropolitan San Francisco. One year I worked doing the cooking; for the other eleven years, I've worked in the gardens.

Now it is my time to be the head gardener. I am responsible for it, and it's responsible for me, so we have a definite connection. I am responsible for organizing the work and for being responsive to the

Green Gulch Farm's ornamental and fruit garden area is on the left, and the fields for market garden crops are at the top and to the right.

life of the garden. This includes working with a lot of different people, both in the community and in our gardening classes for adults and children.

We're cultivating almost fifteen acres now; a big part of this is in cropland, and we also have an acre-and-a-half perennial garden, which is where I concentrate. We grow herbs, flowers, fruits, and vegetables, not only for our community and the Zen Center restaurant and grocery store, but also for the local organic food and restaurant market.

We originally cultivated the land with horses; my husband, Peter, was involved with that. It was challenging and very satisfying. We also had milk cows and chickens. When you begin to enter into the life of animals, it is a big responsibility. It also requires a lot of skill, and we took it very seriously.

But there was a big turnover of people here, and animals don't respond well to that kind of inconsistency. We also had a lot of problems with marauding dogs attacking the chickens, cows, and

A greenhouse filled with many different varieties of lettuce seedlings.

even the horses. We finally decided to give away the animals and started using small machinery, not rototillers but two Japanese Kabota tractors. One is for initial ground preparation—harrowing, disking, and plowing. The other pulls a rig that transplants seedlings and cultivates the row crops.

My major teacher in gardening was the British horticulturist Alan Chadwick, although by the time I met him I'd had a good eight years of gardening under my belt, or as he said, under my fingernails. The way he perceived the plant world and the animal world, and the connection of the human with the plant world, was very much more than just technical gardening. He presented a whole philosophy and spirit of life that I and my closest friends in the garden resonated with tremendously. It was a kind of verification of what we had observed independently.

I didn't have anywhere near the apprenticeship or discipleship with Alan that most of his students did. I only met and worked with him in the last six months of his life, when he was bedridden. What I learned from Alan was much more important to me than any kind of technical information. It was the interconnection between the soil

Lettuce seedlings set out by tractor into the fields.

and human life, how we can nourish and affect each other. He made it very clear that the plant needs the soil just as much as the soil needs the plant, and that was very much corroborated by my experience of working in the garden. Our destinies are tied up together.

The way you work in the garden, the way you walk and carry yourself, the way you look at it, sit in it, breathe in it, observe it, enjoy it, and let yourself be changed by it, is just as important as which crops you decide to plant and bring to market, or any other philosophical view you might have. How you take care of the soil is also really important, and that also fits in with basic meditation.

The key to gardening for me is the connection between the elements, the soil, the human beings working in the soil, and the sky and the air. It is all mixed up in the plants, and it is all a huge mystery offered to us to respond to and digest. I appreciate the opportunity not to demystify the garden, but just to participate in it more.

I love working with all the seemingly paradoxical aspects of gardening. We just did a class teaching people how to make compost out of everything they throw away. It is our least popular class, and yet I feel it is our most important one because we forget that everything changes and even what we discard can become gold, become alive, and nurture life.

Gardening enlivens on other levels as well. I've seen the same kinds of changes happen in people's bodies when they're gardening as happen in the composting process: the conversion of what's no longer useful or vital into something very alive. Although it is hard to find words for this process, I see it again and again and again. I don't know exactly how it happens; I can't describe it, but I'm convinced of the power of this conversion. It is observable, verifiable.

A lot of people come through the Green Gulch Garden who are disturbed either physically or mentally. We've taken on some pretty far-out cases here, and I've seen the healing power of the garden time and time again. Just by giving people a real steady task, and leaving them to do that task, somehow the garden passes through the gardener's hand and mind, and a change happens inside. It's an inexplicable change, an enlivening that I attribute to the garden. As Alan Chadwick described it, "It is not the gardener that makes the garden; it is the garden that makes the gardener."

We're still developing how to offer instruction in gardening. Because we are a meditation community, our whole life isn't only concerned with outreach; it's also very steady internal work. But I've become so convinced of the merit and meaningfulness of working in the earth, that I would want to teach people about gardening no matter where I was. I really feel that my life's work is to share my enthusiasm about gardening.

I am especially interested in working with children. It has been my main focus and interest this year. We have a nine-year-old son who really knows how to work in the garden. All the children here do. I've been working with my son's school class because I find that modern children don't have much of a sense of where their food comes from, and what is actually going on in the garden.

When I asked one child where his food came from, he answered "From the Safeway." I said, "Well, where does the Safeway get it?" He said, "From another Safeway." Many city children haven't had any connection with the earth. I'd like to see us do more work with children, for they are very eager and deeply curious. They're most interested in the compost system and the food crops.

So we have been inviting school classes to come to Green Gulch. I don't have a particular program worked out. It is different each time, although I always show them the garden and let them romp around in it a bit. When they are relaxed enough, and absorbing enough to actually listen, I start to ask them questions. It is a very interactive kind of investigation. We usually do some kind of planting together, such as potatoes, and I show them younger potatoes and exactly how the plant forms its tubers. When they come back for harvesting in the fall, they can see the consequences of their work. It makes it all real. This year some of the parents made a big fire on the beach and after the children harvested their potatoes, they cooked and ate them. They had a sense of the whole life of a potato plant and of its huge contribution to their lives.

We also teach a class in the summer called "Gardening With Your Children," when parents come with their kids. We get a lot of single parents, and a lot of daddies who have their kids for the weekend. We have a big picnic here on the grass after we work. Then we read a story, and harvest some flowers, and do some planting. Sometimes the children gather seed to take home, or they may transplant little lettuces into boxes to take home, so they can observe the results of their labor firsthand. Many say they have actually set up gardens from doing this simple class.

By teaching gardening I'm trying to pay back the kindness of Alan Chadwick and Harry Roberts, another person who taught me. Harry was an eccentric, marvelous human being, raised and trained by the Yurok Indians of the northwest coast of California. He was an excellent agronomist, machinist, and jack-of-all-trades. As a young man in the 1920s, he had driven cattle through the Green Gulch Valley, and forty years later, he was working here with us. He helped us set up our garden, farm, and welding shop. He also was a really good cook, an excellent nurseryman, and a brilliant native plant breeder.

Harry gave us classes every Sunday afternoon. It was not so much, "Here's how you dig; here's how you water," but rather, "Have you noticed what happens when the acacia trees open this time of year rather than a month later? What are the influences that help open them? What are the weather factors that influence growing on the coast? Have you ever wondered why there are those outcroppings of rock up there, and none down here?" For years Harry had us keep records of which plants flowered in the garden and when and what the bloom sequence was. It was a way to develop our awareness of the garden world.

By taking the pulse of your garden, and opening your eyes, you are training your powers of observation and concentration. By keeping a record of the wild plants year after year, you can actually see some patterns that are relevant to gardening in your particular area. If you know intimately the spot where you are living, you can learn from it.

We're doing a lot of work right now on the bottom land near the sea, planting cuttings from cottonwood trees we got from Harry. There are few deciduous trees right in this particular region of the coast, and we need deciduous trees for leaves for the garden and for firewood. Harry suggested we try trees from along the Russian River, Fremont cottonwoods, and black cottonwoods from the Klamath River.

The Fremont cottonwoods died, but not the black cottonwoods. Why? Harry explained that the trees growing in the blast of the salt wind at the mouth of the Klamath River have built up a resistance to their harsh climate over the years, whereas the trees from the Russian River came from a climate that is hotter and more protected. Their leaves got a mold and fungus and blight from the salt wind and heavy fog here at Green Gulch. So this is what I mean by understanding your climate and being able to offer its wisdom to a curious child or adult.

I think a real consequence of our present educational process is that we compartmentalize everything. We break it up into separate subjects and don't trace the whole consequences of our actions. In Buddhism there is a wonderful image of Indra, the chief of the Gods, with a net. At each knotted edge of Indra's net there is a tiny jewel which reflects all the other jewels in the net. That is what I mean by interconnectedness. What is the effect on the whole garden of spraying a particular rose or not spraying it? Being aware of these consequences is an essential aspect of gardening. Gardening can teach us that all parts of our life are very intimately and clearly reflected in Indra's net.

There is very little real work now available to people that makes sense, real graphic believable sense, sense in the broadest meaning of the word. Dealing with the earth and the solid world is believable stuff. If you're a banker, you may not have the same direct sense of what the consequences and the effects of your work are. The world of the banker can be just as deep as the world of the gardener, but I think in the garden it might be easier to feel the depth and consequences of the actions of your life.

There's a T-shirt that has been around for a long time that says, "When the world ceases to satisfy, there's always the garden." And

Beauty for its own sake is not neglected at Green Gulch Farm. In the ornamental garden is a Japanese snowdrop tree (Styrax japonicus) *surrounded by origanum, a carpet of creeping wooly thyme* (Thymus pseudolanuginosus), *thrift* (Armeria), *and catmint* (Nepeta faassenii). *The rose on the background arbor is a Noisette, "Madame Alped Carrier."*

there's a picture of the receding skyline of Manhattan, lost in smoke and smog, with rows and rows of vegetables and smiling gardeners in the foreground. I thought that was a great T-shirt, but then I saw one I love even better. It says, "When the garden ceases to satisfy, there is always the world."

I think that's right; our task is to bring gardens to the world. In my own life I wonder how can I offer all the years of experience that I've had from being a gardener to a tired, unsatisfied world, a world that needs gardens. It is easy to bloom in a garden, but can you actually bloom and help others to bloom in the world? One way is to plant trees and to work with children, and I'm considering other ways of cultivation as well.

There is a lot of talk now about healing the earth. I think this is important. But I think it's as important to heal the human beings who may not understand our earth. In classical Hebrew, the word for soil is "adama," and the word for human being is "ben adam," son of Adam or son of the earth. We have the same root, and can learn to heal ourselves by protecting and developing humus or the soil, by listening to one another, and by being fully human and humane.

Caroline Morrison working in the garden in a Hooker Alley T-shirt.

Caroline Morrison
SOWING COMMUNITY GARDENS

Caroline Morrison loves to garden and has been willing to work very hard so that others can have the chance to garden too. She was one of the founding members of SLUG, the San Francisco League of Urban Gardeners, a nonprofit organization formed to encourage the creation of community gardens throughout that city. Caroline also helped start a community garden of her own on a thin slice of land called Hooker Alley. Each month a member of the garden is interviewed in its newsletter in the section called "Meet Your Fellow Hooker."

178

I was born in Cassoday, a small prairie cow town in the Flint Hills of east central Kansas. That's where the last vestiges of the tallgrass prairie grow—the Big Bluestem prairie grass that used to cover the whole central plains of this country, and fed hordes of buffalo, deer, and antelope.

Cassoday has a population of about one hundred people. Outdoor things were about all there was to do. I had three older brothers who were my role models. Since they spent most of their time outside because they didn't have to do housework, that was, of course, where I wanted to be. As a result I never liked housework, and as I've gotten older I don't like it any better!

My family owned some farm and pastureland, and we had two big gardens, one out a quarter of a mile or so by that farmland, and one at home. As a child, I worked in the garden along with doing other things, such as going after the cows and mowing the lawn and feeding the chickens and working in the hardware store my father owned. But since leaving the family farm, I never had a chance to have a garden of my own; that and the fact that I grew up with an outdoor orientation are why I started this community garden.

In 1978, I was working in San Francisco at the Central YMCA, and I had a project called the ECO Project—Ecology Conservation Opportunity. It involved people from about eighteen to thirty-five or so, doing environmental projects such as repairing trails on Mt. Tamalpais. In return, we would get an environmental education; the leader would give us information about the flora and fauna and history of the areas where we worked. Mostly we did things outside of town, and finally one day the group said, "Why don't we do something in the city?"

I had seen the Fort Mason Community Garden, so I went over to ask how to get something like that started. They told me the city had a Community Garden Project; I called them and asked if they had any places available. There were two spaces left, and I chose a space on Nob Hill called Hooker Alley, a weed-strewn lot filled with ten-foot-high fennel, broken bottles, cans, rocks, trash, and claypan soil. It had been named after either Chester Hooker, a prominent hardware man in the early days of San Francisco, or after "Fighting Joe" Hooker, the Civil War general; no one seems to know for sure.

My ECO group did a lot of the clearing and digging, and I started a garden class that met on Saturdays for a couple of hours. The class would get gardening instruction and then do some work clearing the lot. After six weeks they selected what plot they wanted and got started gardening.

The size of each plot is eight by nine or ten feet, with a few smaller ones and a few larger ones. I was amazed this summer that I actually grew, over the whole season, eighty different varieties in my little plot! I can't grow a lot of things in the winter because my particular plot is the shadiest, but those in the middle can grow quite a bit. However, even the fava beans I planted in my plot this fall for a green manure crop seem to be doing fine.

The gardeners range in age from their thirties into their eighties, but the majority are either seniors or fast approaching it, on fixed or lower incomes. They live within two or three blocks of the garden. Everyone is pretty much responsible for his or her own plot unless they have a special need. For instance, Henry, one of the original gardeners who started in 1978, is in his eighties now, and so we bring compost to his plot and dig it in for him. We did the same for Pat when she broke her elbow.

That's one of the advantages of belonging to a community garden rather than having one in your own backyard; there are friends to help you out when you need an occasional hand to keep on gardening. Another advantage is that it brings neighbors together. People make new friends and learn from each other.

Community gardens also benefit the whole neighborhood. In our case, we cleaned up a ratty-looking old place where winos and thieves used to hang out and made it into an attractive, productive area. We've had a lot of neighbors call out from the apartment building next door to say how much they enjoy the garden, too.

I think Hooker Alley is unique in a few other respects. One, of course, is the location; it's in an area with very little open space, in one of the fanciest neighborhoods in the city. Also, I think it is very unusual for a small community garden—we only have eleven plots—to have our own monthly newsletter and logo and T-shirts. In 1986, we won first prize and four hundred dollars as the Best Small Community Garden in the Western Region in the contest sponsored by the National Community Gardening Association.

We have a real good group at our garden. We have an annual Christmas party and workdays throughout the year when we do the general overall maintenance and share a potluck lunch. We have a lot of fun together. This year we had our second annual tomato-tasting contest, where we judged who grew the largest and best-tasting tomatoes from the twenty-one varieties entered.

A bird's eye view of Hooker Alley Community Garden; the wooden bench also serves as a locker for storing tools.

Much of the success of the garden has been due to volunteers. One of them, Robin Parer, was in my ECO group; she helped teach the gardening class and has continued to give time and energy to the garden. She also edits our monthly newsletter, "Cultivating Hooker Alley." As coordinator of the garden, her help has been invaluable to me as well as to all the gardeners.

We try to encourage using organic methods rather than toxic materials. We relax that a little when it comes to slugs and snails; we do use some snail bait. We have compost bins and everyone is encouraged to add to and take from them as needed. We even won some compost once as a prize in a garden contest! We have a yearly ten-dollar fee to belong to the garden which covers insurance and the supplies we all use, like the hose and wheelbarrow. I'm afraid the fee is going to go up because our insurance costs are increasing.

I obviously enjoy gardening or I wouldn't have done it for over eight years. But sometimes there are things connected with it that make you wonder, why the heck am I doing this? So far, we have had to wage two fights to keep the garden. It was first threatened when the owner of the garage next door wanted to take it over and use Hooker Alley for another entrance. We had to go to the Board of Supervisors and the Planning Commission and the Open Space Committee of the Recreation and Parks Department, and there were quite a few hearings before we got that settled.

Then someone bought the garage and wanted to put up a high-rise building, which we were concerned about due to its height and the shade factor on the garden. The Planning Commission finally approved it but lowered the height; the developer decided it wasn't economically feasible and sold the property again. We are now in the process of trying to change the designation from "street" to "open space," which will give us permanency.

I really get a kick out of planting a seed and seeing it grow, and fresh vegetables taste so much better than the ones in the store, particularly tomatoes. And I enjoy the birds. Fortunately we haven't had pigeons; there is someone in the neighborhood who feeds them on her fire escape, so they just fly over the garden. We have robins and sparrows and doves and hummingbirds. One day, I saw the most exotic bird that I have ever seen in a city. It just startled me. I didn't know what it was so I consulted a bird book and was amazed to discover it was a partridge.

When I started the garden, I was still working full-time, and getting away from the hassles and the pressures of a job were important. I used to walk up here from the "Y" and just sit on the bench and look at the garden and listen to the birds and throw a rock at a mouse and kind of get back to reality, you know, even though I might not have a thing I needed to do in the garden.

There was one gardener who took a plot in the middle of a sticky law suit. She said, "Well, I'm going to spend whatever I have to on this garden because if I don't, I'll spend it on a psychiatrist, and that's a lot more expensive!" One day I came down and found her stretched out on the top of the tool chest; it scared me, and I called to her. She got up, looked at me—she'd been asleep—and said, "You know, this is the first time in six months I've been really relaxed!"

Bob Cantisano in the small greenhouse at Peaceful Valley Farm Supply.

Bob Cantisano
LOOKING AHEAD

Bob Cantisano never abandoned some of the styles or environmental ideals of the sixties. Instead, he deepened his involvement and found ways to make them work, adapting when necessary as times changed. In the seventies he started Peaceful Valley Farm Supply, outside of Nevada City, California. Today it is the oldest organic farm and garden supply in the western United States.

My great aunt and grandfather were both gardeners in Sacramento, and when I was five or six years old, I can remember my mother and father saying, "You have a green thumb," or something to that effect. I gardened a little at home, but not extensively. I grew up in the Bay Area in the fifties and sixties, when vegetable gardening was an oddball sport, but I was always interested in plants, and used to go to the arboretum and the botanical gardens.

I got into farming through the back door. I started out as a manager and then partner in a natural foods store. That store eventually evolved into a large food co-op with a big trucking system because we bought food from all over the West Coast. At first I didn't even know what "organically grown" was. Then, when I became the buyer and met the growers, they explained that it was food grown in fully nourished soils, without the use of chemical fertilizers, pesticides, or herbicides. As time passed, it became clear to me that this was a desirable way to farm. "Earth Day" inspired me, and I started learning about gardening and ecological issues. I was inspired by the farmers I met as well.

My wife is a real hot gardener, and our first major gardening projects together were in Truckee about fifteen years ago, when I was still with the food co-op. Truckee has a real extreme climate, with frost in the summer. We were doing okay, but we didn't know exactly what we were doing; there were a lot of holes in our knowledge. Then we had an opportunity to move with some friends to a piece of land owned by their granddad in the Yuba City area. I was tired of being a businessman and ready for a change, so we decided to see what farming was about.

It turned out to be a lot harder to farm organically than to garden, not just because of the labor involved, but because of the complexity of it, and because we were trying to make a living at it. You've got economic parameters, you've got scale, and the technological systems are not as well developed for large-scale agriculture without chemicals as they have been for gardening.

There was a dearth of information about organic farming, so we had to create our own. It was a slow learning process. But we jumped in with both feet, and fortunately the area is such a naturally fertile zone that even with the mistakes we made, we pulled it off. We actually even made a net profit, which amazed everybody.

Then, in addition to that, we leased an orchard that had thirty different species of trees. At that time the only information about how to grow fruit without commercial pesticides, herbicides, or fertilizers was oriented towards the East Coast. It was really a challenge, and we made some horrendous mistakes. But eventually, we figured it out and were able to grow very good quality fruit without chemicals.

After three years, we moved to lower Nevada County when a really nice piece of land became available. We farmed there for over three years. It was another big challenge because the land was so much less fertile for growing vegetables and flowers. We had to learn again in a new climate and soil type. We grew about six acres of vegetables and managed another hundred acres for hay and pasture and orchard.

People kept coming over and saying, "Hey, you guys know what you are doing." We really didn't, but we were ahead of them. They were so frustrated by the lack of supplier information, and asked so many questions, and were looking for the same stuff we were using, that one day we said, "Why don't we start a little tiny business to see if we can't supply the neighbors?" And that's how Peaceful Valley Farm Supply began.

From the very beginning, our work has been experimental in nature and also "on the fringe" in that it doesn't rely on chemical inputs, and we try to match the natural cycles with the plants' capabilities and our needs. For a long time that was, and still is to a great extent, considered "the fringe." Most of the farming done today is intensively chemical-based and has thirty or forty years of research behind it. There have been very few organic farming or gardening research projects; most of the good information has been passed along by word of mouth or an occasional article. But a lot of times those are general in nature. What we've been doing is figuring out how you make that specific to your site and needs.

Oftentimes, if you just follow general garden rules, you're misled. You can read in garden books that you shouldn't grow broccoli if you're in a hot spring zone, and you should only plant it when temperatures are cool. Around here you can grow broccoli in most places all summer long if you find the right spot. Those are the kinds of things you apply on a site-by-site basis. That's the fun stuff.

I'm too busy with the business to farm right now, but I still garden. We live in a community outside of Nevada City, California, with three other families. We each have our own home, but we share the work of a large garden and other projects that need to be done around the place. About twenty-eight people have about 75 percent of their vegetable needs met by the garden. We sell our surplus, but right now we're mainly growing food and flowers for our own use.

Our goal in our own garden is to make it productive, to have a yield proportionate to the time and money put into it, and still create something beautiful. I can't see any value in putting so much time and money into a garden that the food costs more to produce than if you bought it.

Everyone here knows how to garden and likes it, but I'm the one who probably has the most experience, so I usually initiate projects, and then we work on everything together. It's in order to satiate my curiosity. I'm interested in why things happen, although I also marvel how it all just magically comes about.

I like the challenge of saying, "I got x amount of yield out of this plot last year; how can I get x plus 10 percent? What little trick would give us that extra? If I were just a little smarter here, or more timely there, or picked a different variety, or watered a little differently, or fertilized differently, would that give us that extra little bit?" Those extras are the parts that keep me jazzed up, and drive the science part of my brain.

Besides the day-to-day ongoing experiments, we probably have about ten to twelve specific experiments for our own use, comparing ideas and techniques to see what will fit here. We have cover crop trials and variety trials as well. For example, we have developed a couple of frost-hardy tomatoes; they can survive without any protection down to about 28 degrees.

We also planted eight varieties of cucumbers at the same time to see which will do best in our cold nighttime climate. We have hot days, but as much as a 40- or 50-degree temperature swing at night. That's not particularly conducive to cucumbers, so we're trying to see which varieties will do the best and have the best powdery mildew resistance. We are doing foliar feeding trials on garlic, broccoli, and cauliflower to see how foliar nutrients affect harvest yields and quality. And recently, we did some germination trials, comparing hot water treatment for some seeds with presoaking, presprouting, and even a gel treatment.

We're also trying to figure out how to protect earthworms. We know that rototillers chop them up, so we've been experimenting with rototilling only in the heat of the day and only when the soil is dry because then the earthworms go deeper into the soil.

Another experiment is a comparison between double-dug beds, beds just turned with a garden fork, and rototilled beds. We're doing

An early morning view of the large garden Bob and his wife share with three other couples.

earthworm counts to see what the earthworm population difference is in beds that have been double-dug, rototilled, and not tilled at all, and comparing the time it takes to make each bed up versus the yield and quality differences. That's a real hard one to judge, and we may not have all the data this year, but it is an important question as people like to dig up their gardens differently.

We're looking for products and methods that are cheap, simple, and effective, and which don't poison the environment. One of our goals is to make organic growing as simple as possible, so more people can adopt it. Take the issue of double-digging beds; I work with a lot of older gardeners who can't do that. We know there is an advantage in the raised bed technique because if you have more soil space, you get more plant growth. So we've developed a modified double-digging, where you use a rototiller and just a little bit of shoveling and digging.

We have our entire garden circled in apple trees of many different varieties on different rootstocks to see which ones will do the best. We also have a fire-blight resistance trial to see which varieties are immune to blight without spraying. Commercial farmers spray almost by nature, so they're not so concerned with which plants are naturally susceptible or naturally immune. But we're looking for plants that have natural immunity so gardeners, and especially organic gardeners, don't have to spray even with a natural material.

The plants we can't live with we remove, like Johnson grass, blackberries, or thistles, but we're not concerned that things be weed-free because when you dig up those weeds, you find all kinds of earthworms underneath. Weeds also provide a habitat and a source of food: nectar, pollen, leaves, and seeds for beneficial insects and birds. They are a free source of organic matter, and most soils really need that. Rather than haul a lot of organic matter in, we'd just as soon make it on the site.

I share the results of our experiments through my business because we give farmers and gardeners advice when they purchase our supplies; it comes out as another set of instructions or directions that we've researched. Our role is to help people avoid failures, so that the novice can get to be the beginner, the beginner can get to be the intermediate, and the intermediate can become the expert. I consider myself an intermediate gardener—I'm working toward expertise. But in the process, I'm helping those novices and beginners experience such success that they'll want to keep on growing. As we and others succeed, the process becomes more established and moves into the mainstream.

In the last four or five years, organic gardening has started to become an accepted, even trendy thing to do, but organic growing hasn't caught on much in the farm world yet. There are more organic farmers than ever before, but it's still a small percentage. In spite of that, our organic farm supply business has grown at a phenomenal rate; we've been averaging a 50 percent or greater growth for the last four years. We've grown from a one person part-time job to a full-scale business with eleven employees.

Now I'm looking for someone to either sell it to or to come in as a partner because it is growing past my management abilities. I don't have the business background to handle that kind of growth. I want to go back to doing more full-time farming and gardening research work. Right now, time-wise I'm already maxed out; I don't even have the time I want for my family, much less the other work I want to do. The next stage in the business is to make a big jump forward to satisfy its growth potential, and if I did that, I would be committed to improving the business for another five to ten years.

I tend to be the starter of projects. It has been my nature for a long time. We were among the first people to ever do the intensive planting system, what's called biodynamic French intensive gardening now. We developed that system about the same time as Alan Chadwick and John Jeavons. A lot of our fertilizing practices are now commonplace. We kept looking for inexpensive materials that would work well in the Sierra foothills, and developed a fertilizer blend based on a common soil type here that is now used by probably thousands of gardeners.

Number-wise, gardeners are the most active part of our business, but my major area of focus, and the biggest challenge, has been with farmers. There we are working to make a major change ecologically and sociologically. Right now, farming is a man-made disaster. There is very little that is ecologically sound in present commercial agricultural practices; yet most farmers haven't realized that they have other options.

So we can make a dent in two ways. The first is to reduce the demand on the system by having more gardeners growing their own food, flowers, and herbs. Also gardeners tend not to have the pest problems that farmers do, so they don't use as much pesticide.

Second, we can help those farmers who are interested learn how to farm organically. I help the larger growers develop cost-effective fertilization and pest control practices that don't rely on chemicals. Seven or eight years ago I sought farmers out, but now we don't have to solicit business; it comes to us as fast as we can handle it. Articles have been written up about our work or someone requests our catalog or people hear about us at workshops and through personal referrals. I occasionally speak. Last night, for example, I talked to a horse owners association about how to get off using pesticides for fly control and worming animals. Most of the people in that room were not already convinced—they were there to learn.

I am better and better received at those events as time goes on. The ideas that were obviously on the fringe fifteen or twenty years ago have started to hit home. You don't have to have too many Kesterson Reservoirs, or contaminated and closed wells, or Bhopal, Indias, or watermelon poisonings, or Chernobyls for all this to ring true in the mainstream. And it's about time!

Even if they weren't concerned about disasters, many farmers are no longer succeeding with the agricultural techniques of the last forty years. They're going broke, they've got health problems, they've got wells which are contaminated, pesticides which don't work, fertilizer that costs more than ever, and higher pumping costs because the land won't hold water any more. No longer are these people saying to me, "You're off the wall." For many it's, "Maybe I'm not ready for it myself, but I'll find out as much about it as I can."

Just look at the issue of pesticides. They're more expensive than ever, they're less effective than ever, there are fewer new ones coming onto the market than ever, they have more known environmental hazards than ever. There is a shift taking place right now that is hard to quantify, but you can see it in the interest level in our business and in the increased interest in the whole process of organic growing.

We're hoping that we can help these commercial farmers become successful enough to act as a model for the rest of the mainstream people who have not yet seen the need. The organic farmers in many communities are still considered the oddballs, and they're not looked at over the fence too much as models. We want to

Weeds are allowed to flourish because they bring nutrients to the soil's surface that are then added to the soil when the weeds are composted.

give the commercial farmer enough successful ideas to be able to start someplace up the ladder instead of at ground level, and not go out of business as he or she learns. That's why I keep doing research and why we have research projects going on with the farmers we work with. Also, we keep trying to push the University of California to do more organically oriented research projects.

With the increased interest people have in more healthy eating and life styles, organic growing is spreading. The gourmet food trend of California cuisine is also based on organically grown food, although most of the people in those expensive restaurants don't know they're eating organic food. Right now we have supermarkets interested in organically grown food for the first time. If we can prove that it is successful in a couple of major supermarkets, that will act as an impetus for other ones to look over their shoulders and see that it is going to be a viable idea. This, in turn, will encourage more farmers to practice ecological methods.

I think the biggest difference between organic farming and chemical farming is that you replace inputs with intelligence. When you don't use chemicals, you have to become a more intelligent grower because you have to understand the ecosystem better and how you fit into it. If you buy chemicals out of a bag, you don't have to pay as much attention to that. What are the conditions that cause pest outbreaks, and what are the variables that cause fertility increase or decrease? Our biggest role is to provide that knowledge. We have products that fit into that system, but what we're doing is providing people with the impetus and ideas so they don't need to buy any products, natural or not.

In fact, that's a pretty interesting problem. Our business is growing radically because there is such an increased interest. But if I looked at how much money an individual farmer spent with our business, we could never survive on individual farmers because what we're showing them is how to need fewer inputs and spend less money. I have customers now that I've had for ten years that I don't sell one tenth as much to as I did, and they're doing better than ever, at far less cost.

I think that's great, because what we're trying to do is give people a proper idea, and if they need a product, fine, we've got an option for them, but if they don't need to buy anything, that's even better. A lot of our customers use us mostly as an information source. One day I took out a notepad and started scratching down the number of questions I'd answered that day; it was in excess of two hundred fifty. We're now trying to put a lot of this information into a computer. I also teach seminars and classes, and we share a lot of our information through pamphlets.

I've been to hundreds and hundreds of farms and gardens as a consultant, and have had an opportunity to see different systems evolve. Every time I do that, I pick up as much as I give. I'm a gatherer, a vacuum cleaner for information. What I bring to each farm is a vision of what the end product could look like and how we should get from point A to Z.

If I can make something simple and ecologically sound and economically viable, people will adopt it. For example, apple trees have a significant problem with the codling moth: it lays eggs that turn into little worms in the apples. Home growers might have as much as 80 percent of their apples damaged by the codling moth larvae. You need to spray for it three or four times a year if you're using commercial chemicals. Organic sprays are more short-lived in the environment, so you have to spray even more than that. Most gardeners just don't get around to doing all that, so they get wormy apples.

About fifteen years ago, I started playing around with pheromone traps, to trap the moth before it lays its eggs. I finally found a great system that works! Now, for the five minutes a month it takes to put one trap in each tree, you get worm-free apples. That's what we want: something simple and ecological that works. I've got a company now that makes these things, and it's making a fair living. Those are the kinds of projects we want to keep doing.

It has been interesting to watch my folks' reaction to all this. They were real disgruntled that I didn't go on to college. I had the ability and intelligence, but I wasn't interested in school. I love to do hands-on work. My wife and I have lived a pretty alternative life style, once in a place with no electricity, sixteen miles down a dirt road. They were worried that I wasn't doing something productive with my life, and thought, boy, these kids are really way out. And what are they doing to our grandchildren?

But they see that we're making a living, and now we've adopted a slightly more mainstream life style. They no longer think that I'm on the fringe, and they see that the ideas I was raving about fifteen years ago are finally settling into the larger society. They have even started to garden more themselves!

Which reminds me of something else. There are a lot more gardeners now than I've ever seen before. As a rule, they seem to be increasing both the quality and quantity of what they're growing. They're increasing the area that they're planting in, and that's from being successful. It's also interesting that a big portion of our new customers and gardeners are over fifty years old. In the early years they were almost all people in their twenties and thirties.

I think a garden is one of the most socially helpful trends at present. I've never found a true gardener who represented the violent section of society. Gardening and violence don't cross over, or if they do, it is very little. Gardening is healthful and peaceful. It helps heal the earth and its gardeners. The more people we can get out there working in the dirt and having success and feeling proud of what they're doing, the more it makes an impact on other people and the world. But I'm also pretty pragmatic. I want to make sure that what we do is worthwhile in a dollars and cents way.

I'm interested in healthy food, for myself and my family, and a healthy life style. I like that our four children have a healthy place to live and play and work. We make sure that our soils are really well mineralized and have all the nutrients necessary for fully nourished food. Gardening is also the best day-to-day exercise that I do. It is much more fun than jogging or bicycling because it's productive, and I like getting something done for more people than just myself.

Gardening is a challenge, and I like having to pay attention to what I'm doing while I'm doing it. Gardening also recharges me, and clears out my head. I focus on the positive things and the day-to-day hassles get left behind. It makes me feel that I'm contributing, that I'm growing as a person.

I get a sense that I'm part of the ecosystem. That's really important to me because I grew up in the city. I like to teach the kids, so I bring them out into the garden and say, "Here are the butterflies, here are the eggs they lay, here are the worms that hatch out, and here are the bugs that eat them. Do you see the dynamics of the whole process?" That's the kind of stuff that makes the world go around, I think. For a long time I didn't understand that, but the more time I spent out there, the more it became obvious to me.

I like to work with living things, to see something grow to its maturity and fulfill itself. And I like to do things to their best—that is something you can really achieve in a garden. But I also garden because I love it. I like the color and beauty. I like the bugs cruising through. I like the birds in the morning. I like the earthworms and the smell of the soil. I like to be outside. I like the sun on my face. I like the hard work and the easy work.

I like running through the sprinklers to cool off. I'm just as jazzed now about standing in the sprinklers on a hot day as I was fifteen years ago, except that now as I stand in them I look out and say, "I'm doing a lot better than I was then." I can see that we are actually finally making a change.

I talked to one of my cherry growers the other day, a guy who has been farming for thirty-five years. He said, "This is the best cherry crop I've ever had." That's an encouraging sign. It makes me feel really good. It is real satisfying to sit down to eat our garden's harvest, with our flowers on the table, after a good day working in the soil and with some positive feedback from our customers.

Someone once told me it was the wave theory. The first wave crashes on the beach and the next one rolls in behind it. We're in that first wave. We always have been. But the first wave is starting to become the second wave. I think the second wave is the really critical one. If that second wave of farmers and gardeners succeeds, then the mass will come, and the planet will have a real chance to heal itself and provide bounty for all beings. I'm looking forward to a healthier, happier future.

Mixed flower border at Green Gulch Farm; all except the rose were started from seed. In the foreground are low growing foliage and blooms of Veronica teucrium, *while behind are massed plantings of yellow columbine* (Aquilegia chrysantha) *mixed with* Delphinium bellamosum. *The trellised rose is* Rosa soulianna.

Appendix

Bob and Olive Shepherd's compost pile in a corner of their vegetable garden that is ringed with fruit trees.

Pesticides

PERHAPS because my family was involved in ranching and farming for many years, I am concerned about the safety of pesticides from the standpoint of farmers and farm workers as well as gardeners and consumers. Unfortunately, health problems among farming families are starting to surface. For example, in studies done in Texas and New York, agricultural workers have been found to be at increased risk for testicular cancer.[1] In a case control study in Iowa and Minnesota, increased risk of leukemia was found to be associated with herbicide and insecticide use.[2] In Kansas, farmers exposed to herbicides more than twenty days per year had a sixfold increase in risk for non-Hodgkin's lymphoma.[3]

Because I am not an expert in this field, I have borrowed the most clearly written, succinct information that I could find about pesticides in general from other sources. This information provides a thumbnail sketch of the problems we have created for ourselves and for generations to come. Some organizations working to solve them have been listed in the Resources section for those readers who wish to become more actively involved.

---

1. Mills, P.K., Newell, G.R., "Testicular cancer risk in agricultural occupations," *Journal of Occupational Medicine*, 26:798-799, 1984. See also Mills, P.K., Newell, G.R., Johnson, D.E., "Testicular cancer associated with exployment in agriculture and oil and natural gas extraction," *Lancet*, 1:207-210, 1984.

2. Blair, A., Everett G., Cantor, K., "Leukemia and farm practices," *American Journal of Epidemiology*, 122:535, 1985.

3. Hoar, S., Blair, A., Holmes, F., Boysen, C., Robel, R. Hoover, R., Fraumeni, J., "Agricultural herbicide use and risk of lymphoma and soft tissure sarcoma," *Journal of American Medicine*, September 5, 1986, Vol. 256, No. 9, pp. 1141-1146.

Pesticides—An Overview

The material below is the most clear and succinct description for the layperson I could find of our pesticide predicament. It is excerpted from Pesticide Alert, *by Lawrie Mott and Karen Snyder of the Natural Resources Defense Council, and published by Sierra Club Books. I am deeply grateful to them for allowing this information to be reprinted almost in its entirety. The whole book is worth reading.*

EACH YEAR approximately 2.6 billion pounds of pesticides are used in the United States.[1] Pesticides are applied in countless ways, not just on food crops. They are sprayed on forests, lakes, city parks, lawns, and playing fields, and in hospitals, schools, offices, and homes. They are also contained in a huge variety of products from shampoos to shelf paper, mattresses to shower curtains. As a consequence, pesticides may be found wherever we live and work, in the air we breathe, in the water we drink, and in the food we eat. A former director of the federal government's program to regulate pesticides called these chemicals the number one environmental risk, because all Americans are exposed to them.[2]

By definition, pesticides are toxic chemicals—toxic to insects, weeds, fungi, and other unwanted pests. Most are potentially harmful to humans and can cause cancer, birth defects, changes in genetic material that can be inherited by the next generation (genetic mutations), and nerve damage, among other debilitating or lethal effects. Many more of these chemicals have not been thoroughly tested to identify their health effects.

Pesticides applied in agriculture—the production of food, animal feed, and fiber, such as cotton—account for 60 percent of all U.S. pesticide use other than disinfectants and wood preservatives.[3] Pesticides are designed to control or destroy undesirable pests. Insecticides control insects; herbicides control weeds; fungicides control fungi such as mold and mildew; and rodenticides control rodents. Some of these chemicals are applied to control pests that reduce crop yields or to protect the nutritional value of our food; others are used for cosmetic purposes to enhance the appearance of fresh food.

As a result of massive agricultural applications of pesticides, our food, drinking water, and the world around us now contain pesticide residues; they are literally everywhere, in the United States and throughout the world. In fact, though all these chemicals have been banned from agricultural use, nearly all Americans have residues of the pesticides DDT, chlordane, heptachlor, aldrin, and dieldrin in their bodies.[4] Ground water is the source of drinking water for 95 percent of rural Americans and 50 percent of all Americans. Yet, according to a 1987 Environmental Protection Agency (EPA) report, at least 20 pesticides, some of which cause cancer and other harmful effects, have been found in ground water in at least 24 states.[5] In California alone, 57 different pesticides have been detected in the ground water.[6] The banned pesticide DBCP remains in 2,499 drinking water wells in California's San Joaquin Valley—1,473 of these contaminated wells are not considered suitable for drinking water or bathing because the DBCP levels exceed the state health department's action level.[7] As more states conduct ground water sampling programs for pesticides, more pesticides are expected to be found. Surface water supplies have been found to contain pesticides. For example, the herbicide alchlor, or Lasso, has contaminated both ground and surface water in the Midwest, primarily as a result of use on corn and soybeans. Meanwhile, the federal government provides financial assistance to cotton and soybean farmers because enormous surpluses of these crops exist in the United States.

The extent of contamination of our food is unknown. The Federal Food and Drug Administration (FDA) monitors our food supply to detect pesticide residues. Between 1982 and 1985, the FDA detected pesticide residues in 48 percent of the most frequently consumed fruits and vegetables. This figure probably understates the presence of pesticides in food because about half of the pesticides applied to food cannot be detected by the FDA's routine laboratory methods, and the FDA samples less than one percent of our food.[8]

The cumulative effect of widespread, chronic low level exposure to pesticides is only partially understood. Some of the only examples now available involve farmers and field workers. A National Cancer Institute study found that farmers exposed to herbicides had a six times greater risk than nonfarmers of contracting one type of cancer.[9] Other studies have shown similar results, with farmers exposed to pesticides having an increased risk of developing cancer.[10] Researchers at the University of Southern California uncovered startling results in a 1987 study sponsored by the National Cancer Institute. Children living in homes where household and garden pesticides were used have as much as a sevenfold greater chance of developing childhood leukemia.[11]

Another frightening consequence of the long-term and increasing use of pesticides is that the pest species farmers try to control are becoming resistant to these chemicals. For example, the number of species resistant to insecticides nearly doubled between 1970 and 1980.[12] Resistance among weeds and fungi has also risen sharply in the last two decades. In order to combat this problem, greater amounts of pesticides must be applied to control the pest, which in turn can increase the pest's resistance to the chemical. For example, since the 1940s pesticide use has increased tenfold, but crop losses to insects have doubled.[13]

Pesticides can also have detrimental effects on the environment. The widespread use of chlorinated insecticides, particularly DDT, significantly reduced bird populations, affecting bald eagles, ospreys, peregrine falcons, and brown pelicans. DDT is very persistent and highly mobile in the environment. Animals in the Antarctic and from areas never sprayed have been found to contain DDT or its metabolites.[14] Though most of the organochlorines are no longer used in the United States, continuing use in other nations has serious environmental consequences. Other types of pesticides now applied in the United States have adverse effects on the environment. . . .

A February 1987 EPA report, entitled *Unfinished Business*, ranked pesticides in food as one of the nation's most serious health and environmental problems.[15] . . . To date, the EPA has identified 55 cancer causing pesticides that may leave residues in food.[16] Other pesticides can cause birth defects or miscarriages. Some pesticides can produce changes in the genetic material, or genetic mutations, that can be passed to the next generation. Other pesticides can cause sterility or impaired fertility.

Under today's scientific practices, predictions of the potential adverse effects of chemicals on humans are based on laboratory testing in animals. Unfortunately, the overwhelming majority of pesticides used today have not been sufficiently tested for their health hazards. The National Academy of Sciences estimated, by looking at a selected number of chemicals, that data to conduct a thorough assessment of health effects were available for only 10 percent of the ingredients in pesticide products used today.[17]

A 1982 Congressional report estimated that between 82 percent and 85 percent of pesticides registered for use had not been adequately tested for their ability to cause cancer; the figure was 60 percent to 70 percent for birth defects, and 90 percent to 93 percent for genetic mutations.[18] This situation has occurred because the majority of pesticides now available were licensed for use before the EPA established requirements for health effects testing.

In 1972, Congress directed the EPA to reevaluate all these older chemicals (approximately 600) by the modern testing regimens. Through reregistration, the EPA would fill the gaps in required toxicology tests. Roughly 400 pesticides are registered for use on food, and 390 of these are older chemicals that are undergoing reregistration review.[19] By 1986, however, the EPA still had not completed a final safety reassessment for any of these chemicals. To make matters worse, scientists are uncovering new types of adverse health effects caused by chemicals. For example, a few pesticides have been found to damage components of the immune system—the body's defense network to protect against infections, cancer, allergies, and autoimmune diseases.[20] Yet testing for toxicity to the immune system is not part of the routine safety evaluation for chemicals. In short, pesticides are being widely used with virtually no knowledge of their potential long-term effects on human health and the human population is unknowingly serving as the test subject.

The lack of health effects data on pesticides means that the EPA is regulating pesticides out of ignorance, rather than knowledge. This poses particularly serious consequences for the EPA's regulation of pesticides in food. Pesticides may only be applied to a food crop after the EPA has established a maximum safe level, or tolerance, for pesticide residues in food. However, the EPA's tolerances may permit unsafe levels of pesticides for five reasons:

1. EPA established tolerances without necessary health and safety data.

2. EPA relied on outdated assumptions about what constitutes an average diet, such as assuming we eat no more than 7.5 ounces per year of avocado, artichokes, melon, mushrooms, eggplants, or nectarines, when

setting tolerance levels.

3. Tolerances are rarely revised when new scientific data about the risks of a pesticide are received by the EPA.

4. Ingredients in pesticides that may leave hazardous residues in food, such as so-called "inert" ingredients, are not considered in tolerance setting.

5. The EPA's tolerances allow carcinogenic pesticide residues to occur in food, even though no "safe" level of exposure to a carcinogen may exist.

The EPA is not solely responsible for the flaws in the federal government's program to protect our food supply. The FDA monitors food to ensure that residue levels do not exceed the EPA's tolerances. Food containing pesticide residues in excess of the applicable tolerance violates the food safety law and the FDA is required to seize this food in order to prevent human consumption. However, the FDA is not always capable of determining which foods have illegal pesticide residues. For instance, the FDA's routine laboratory methods can detect fewer than half the pesticides that may leave residues in food. Some of the pesticides used extensively on food that cannot be regularly identified include alachlor, benomyl, daminozide, and the EBDCs (ethylene bidithiocarbamates, the most widely used fungicides in the United States). Furthermore, the FDA's enforcement against food with residues in excess of tolerance levels is ineffective; according to a 1986 General Accounting Office report, for 60 percent of the illegal pesticide residue cases identified, the FDA did not prevent the sale or the ultimate consumption of the food. . . .[21]

To understand the potential risks associated with pesticide residues in food, consider the case of the pesticide captan. This chemical is widely used on fruits and vegetables, and is a common residue in food. Although the levels of captan usually found in food are below the EPA's tolerances, even these residues may not be safe for four reasons: First, the EPA has called this chemical a probable human carcinogen; therefore any level of exposure may cause cancer. Second, the majority of captan tolerances were set before the EPA knew the chemical caused cancer. Third, the tolerances do not cover one of the compound's breakdown products that may also be a carcinogen. Fourth, the EPA's determinants of what levels of captan in food should be acceptable do not consider exposure to captan through nonfood sources such as paints, mattresses, shower curtains, and shampoos. Although the EPA began a special review of this chemical in 1980 because of

concerns about its hazards, by 1987 the Agency still had taken no steps to restrict the use of the chemical or protect the public. . . .

Exposure to any level of pesticide residues is also cause for concern because the possibility of synergism exists. Synergism is when the simultaneous exposure to more than one toxic chemical produces a greater toxic effect than the straight sum of the chemicals' individual toxicities. Each fruit or vegetable may contain more than one kind of pesticide, and an entire meal of different foods may expose us to several different pesticides.

1. EPA, Office of Pesticide Programs, "Pesticide Industry Sales and Usage 1985 Market Estimates," Table 4, September 1986.

2. Phil Shabecoff, "Pesticide Control Finally Tops the EPA's List of Most Pressing Problems," *New York Times*, March 6, 1986.

3. EPA, Office of Pesticide Programs, "Pesticide Industry Sales and Usage 1985 Market Estimates," Table 3, September 1986.

4. Robert S. Murphy, *et al.*, "Selected Pesticide Residues or Metabolites in Blood and Urine Specimens from a General Population Survey," *Environmental Health Perspectives*, 48:81-86, 1983.

5. EPA, *Agricultural Chemicals in Ground Water Strategic Plan*, June 1987.

6. David Cohen and Gerald Bowes, *Water Quality and Pesticides: A California Risk Assessment Program*, California Water Resources Control Board, December 20, 1984, with February 26, 1985 update.

7. Ibid.

8. GAO, *Pesticides: Need to Enhance FDA's Ability to Protect the Public from Illegal Residues*, October 1986.

9. Shelia Hoar, *et al.*, "Agricultural Herbicide Use and Risk of Lymphoma and Soft Tissue Sarcoma," *Journal of American Medical Association*, 256:1141-1147, 1986.

10. Aaron Blair, *et al.*, "Leukemia Among Nebraska Farmers: A Death Certificate Study," *American Journal of Epidemiology*, 110:264-273, 1979; Leon Burmeister, *et al.*, "Selected Cancer Mortality

and Farm Practices in Iowa," *American Journal of Epidemiology*, 118:72-77, 1983.

11. Ruth Lowengart, *et al.*, "Childhood Leukemia and Parents' Occupational and Home Exposures," *Journal of National Cancer Institute*, 79:39-46, 1987.

12. Michael Dover and Brian Croft, *Getting Tough: Public Policy and the Management of Pesticide Resistance*, World Resources Institute, p. 7, November 1984.

13. David Pimental, *et al.*, "Benefits and Costs of Pesticide Use in the U.S. Food Production," *Bioscience*, 28:772-784, December 1978.

14. Gino Marco, *et al.*, Editor, *Silent Spring Revisited*, American Chemical Society, p. 94, 1987.

15. EPA, *Unfinished Business: A Comparative Assessment of Environmental Problems*, February 1987.

16. National Academy of Sciences, *Regulating Pesticides in Food: The Delaney Paradox*, 1987.

17. National Academy of Sciences, *Toxicity Testing: Strategies to Determine Needs and Priorities*, 1984.

18. *EPA Pesticide Regulatory Program Study*, House Committee on Agriculture, Subcommittee on Department Operations, Research, and Foreign Agriculture, 97th Congress, 2nd Session 1982.

19. GAO, *Pesticides: EPA's Formidable Task to Assess and Regulate Their Risks*, April 1986.

20. Leon Olson, "The Immune System and Pesticides," *Journal of Pesticide Reform*, Summer 1986.

21. GAO, *Pesticides: Need to Enhance FDA's Ability to Protect the Public from Illegal Residues*, October 1986.

The Safety of Pesticides

The following material on the safety of pesticides has been drawn from an essay titled "The Hidden Health Effects of Pesticides" by Marty Strange, Liz Krupicka, and Dan Looker, from the excellent publication It's Not All Sunshine and Fresh Air: Chronic Health Effects of Modern Farming Practices, *published by The Center for Rural Affairs in Walthill, Nebraska, 68067. The information has been paraphrased and condensed, but the authors deserve all the credit for the research involved and for their willingness to share it.*

MODERN science has created tens of thousands of pesticides. In the United States today, about two thousand are currently in use, with the top forty-three accounting for 80 percent of the usage.[1] The pesticides most commonly used in agriculture work either as growth regulators of pests or on their nervous systems.

In order to sell, ship, or deliver a pesticide in this country, it must be registered by the Environmental Protection Agency (EPA). Registration is supposed to occur only after it has been determined that the pesticide will perform as intended without causing "any unreasonable risk to man or to the environment, taking into account the economic, social and environmental costs and benefits. . . ."

In deciding what is and is not a reasonable risk, the EPA must balance two interests: the need to control pests that compete with people for food crops by means of chemicals in which there is a substantial financial interest, and the health of the human population and the environment. It is taken for granted that these interests are at odds, and that there will be a health risk "cost" to individuals and society by using them. The EPA tries to weigh the benefits of chemical use against these costs, and to determine to what extent a chemical can be used without the costs exceeding the benefits.

The EPA requires a variety of studies to determine health and environmental risks. Initial studies of acute toxicity determine the immediate effects of swallowing, touching, or inhaling the pesticide; the results are displayed on the warning labels of pesticide products. The next level of studies, called subchronic, determines the possible long-term effects of exposure to the chemical for short periods. These studies usually indicate which organs in the body might be affected by the chemical, and the size of the dosage required to test for long-term chronic effects—the final level of studies. Tests for chronic effects determine the long-term effects of repeated exposure in small doses over a long period of time: whether or not the chemical causes cancer, alters gene structure, damages the reproductive system, causes stillbirths or birth defects, or damages the nervous system.

The risk which a chemical poses to users and society should be weighed against the benefit it brings, that is, whether or not it performs effectively. The EPA used to require that efficacy tests be performed to show whether a chemical being registered actually did what its manfacturers claimed it would do. In 1979, the EPA issued regulations temporarily waiving these efficacy tests, and has now proposed rules which would make the waiver of these tests permanent. The EPA's rationale is that farmers and other users would not buy products which did not work, and if they did, the manufacturer is potentially liable for damage suits. Using consumers to determine the efficacy of potentially dangerous products has not been an acceptable policy of other regulatory agencies such as the Food and Drug Administration (FDA).

Because it assumes that every chemical marketed is effective, the EPA must then only determine whether the benefits from use exceed the cost of the health risk which society assumes when people and the environment are exposed to it. This cost-benefit analysis is done only on pesticides which tests have revealed to be relatively high risk. The benefit is calculated as the economic loss to society of banning the use of the chemical, based on the extent of its use and the existence of safer substitutes. The cost is measured in potential loss of life and projected health and medical costs.

A very serious flaw in the process is that the tests done to evaluate the health risks of chemicals considered for EPA registration are not done by independent scientists. They are done by the manufacturers who want to register the chemical, or by laboratories the manufacturers hire to do the tests. In addition, according to the Federal Insecticide, Fungicide, and Rodenticide Act, the results should be accessible to the public, but they have not been since 1979.

That year, a major pesticide manufacturer, Monsanto Co., filed suit against the EPA to prevent it from releasing information to the public about the health effects of its pesticide glyphosate. Monsanto claimed that since it had paid for the health effects research, that research was therefore its property and the government had no right to release it to the public. Monsanto also argued that the information gathered by these studies might be used by its competitors, and therefore should be given trade secret status.

A federal district court agreed, and an injunction was issued prohibiting EPA from releasing such data *on any chemical*. Only the EPA and reviewers chosen by the agency can see test data and analysis, thus protecting them from the scrutiny of independent scientists, a highly unusual policy in light of the potential public health hazards involved and the peer review and publication requirements normally associated with professional science. The EPA has appealed this decision to the Supreme Court and the case is pending.

Instead of independent, rigorous scientific

quality controls, the federal pesticide regulatory system has relied upon the goodwill, integrity, and honesty of pesticide manufacturers and the laboratories they hire to provide test studies. The inherent potential conflict of interest in this policy increases the risk that shoddy or deceptive findings might be used to support erroneous conclusions about a chemical's safety. That is exactly what happened in 1977 when an EPA audit of Industrial Bio-Test Laboratories (IBT), a commercial testing laboratory specializing in pesticide registration tests, revealed massive fraud. Nearly 75 percent (594) of the 801 major studies done in support of 140 chemical registrations were found to be invalid.

It had been a routine practice to falsify test results and fabricate data on major health effects studies. This scandal threw into question the credibility of the registration process itself, and, of course, the safety of pesticides on the market. More than 25 percent (45 of 163) of the health effects studies conducted for registration of the ten leading herbicides and five leading insecticides used in midwestern agriculture were done by IBT, and all but one of the IBT studies were invalid. Only five chemicals were registered solely on the basis of IBT tests, but the registrations of 140 chemicals had been based on some of these invalid IBT tests, creating huge gaps in the chronic health effects data of these chemicals.

In spite of these revelations, none of these chemicals' registrations was suspended or revoked. Many of these pesticides are now undergoing the process of being re-registered by the EPA, and the EPA and the FDA have established a laboratory audit program to spot-check testing laboratories and assure high standards for research on health effects. However, the EPA has not changed its general policy regarding independent research, and the public still does not have access to chronic health effects information.

In addition, there are serious gaps in the health effects studies of chemicals which have been on the market for a long time because at the time they were registered, outdated testing procedures and analytical methods were used. Also, some were registered when health effects test requirements were not as rigorous as they are today. A congressional subcommittee reviewed the files of sixty active chemical ingredients and found that only 52 percent of the presently required cancer studies, 62 percent of the birth defect studies, and 52 percent of the reproductive impairment studies were on file with the EPA.[2]

To fill these gaps, EPA has instituted a re-registration process in which each currently registered chemical is to be re-examined according to current scientific standards for evaluating health effects. Because of the large number of chemicals involved and the time it takes for this process to be completed, some chemicals will not be re-registered until the next century. Meanwhile, the use and sale of pesticides on which the EPA has inadequate chronic health effects data continue.

If the data gathered indicate that the risks outweigh the benefits and there may be an "unreasonable adverse effect" on people or on the environment, the EPA then conducts a "Special Review." The burden is on the EPA, however, to prove its case before taking any action to restrict that chemical—a process that often takes many years.

During this process, the EPA analyzes the scientific data to calculate public exposure to the pesticide, estimates the risk to the public and the environment, and considers this risk against the benefits of continued use. An initial position is established and published under the title "Position Document No. 1" and 105 days are allowed for public comment. Since, however, the public does not have access to this data, this time period is used primarily by manufacturers to present rebuttal information.

The EPA then either drops its stated concerns in Position Document No. 2 or specifies the corrective action that needs to be taken in Position Document No. 3. This can include cancellation of registration,

reclassification, restricting the product's uses, or changing its labeling requirements, which usually means changing the product chemically. The full record is sent to a Science Advisory Panel and the Department of Agriculture for review, and again, public comment is solicited. Since the public still does not have access to this information, participation is generally limited to the registrant, its competitors, the United States Department of Agriculture (USDA), the Science Advisory Panel, and the EPA. Occasionally, environmental groups intervene.

An important key to the success of this process is the initial determination that a chemical warrants a Special Review. In this area the EPA has come under considerable criticism. A congressional committee staff investigation recently concluded that policy changes within the EPA have had the effect of lowering the public guard against pesticides which may cause cancer because the EPA now:

- Allows a test which shows positive findings of a cancer risk to be offset by a number of negative tests. "Limited evidence of risk" is equated with limited risk.

- Uses mutagenicity tests to decide whether a chemical which is cancer causing in animals also affects the animal's genetic structure; if it does not, its risk of causing human cancer is considered less serious.

- Has increased the level of risk of cancer which is considered "tolerable." Risks ten to one hundred times greater than those previously accepted are now considered tolerable.

- No longer considers a significant increase in benign, non-cancerous tumors as sufficient evidence to trigger special review.

This process sounds relatively straight-forward, but it can become quite complicated, as illustrated by the case of trifluralin, an herbicide used extensively for weed control in soybeans, cotton, and other crops. Trifluralin is the active chemical ingredient in the herbicide

Treflan, made by Elanco Products Co., a division of Eli Lilly. It has been preferred by farmers for many years because it does not remain in the soil and adversely affect subsequent crops planted in rotation.

By 1977, however, it was learned that nitrosamines, highly carcinogenic compounds, were present in trifluralin. The nitrosamine of most concern was N-nitroso-di-n-propylamine, or NDPA. Petitions were filed by environmental groups and some members of Congress to suspend Treflan's registration, and in 1979, the EPA ordered a Special Review of all pesticides containing trifluralin.

In the initial review, the EPA decided that the amount of NDPA in trifluralin had to be reduced to one part per million. Before the studies for cancer, reproductive impairment, mutation, and birth defects had been carried out, however, Elanco notified the EPA that rats fed nearly pure trifluralin (with less than one part per million of NDPA) developed significantly increased rates of cancer in their kidneys, bladders, and thyroid glands. In addition, it was discovered that NDPA was not the only nitrosamine in trifluralin; two others, called C7 and C8 nitrosamines for the number of carbon atoms in each, were present and they were more carcinogenic than NDPA.

The initial risk analysis was therefore invalid, but the EPA meanwhile approved registration of Treflan for additional uses in weed control in barley and grain sorghum. The manufacturer had reduced the NDPA contamination level in Treflan from five parts per million to 0.01 parts per million, so the EPA concluded that risk to the public had been reduced to a level almost too small to measure. Using Treflan samples which showed C7/C8 contamination at 0.02 parts per million, it concluded that risk from this source was very low. At the same time, it concluded that the risk of cancer from exposure to trifluralin itself was much higher than previously thought, but because it considered the risk still to be only about one in a million, the EPA found that "The overall risk had not changed signifi-

cantly . . ." and that "the added risk due to exposure to trifluralin is offset by the reduction of NDPA . . ."

Then, inexplicably, the EPA decided to permit manufacturers to let the level of all nitrosamines in trifluralin reach 0.5 parts per million, roughly two and a half times the level that was used in its analysis of cancer risks. NDPA is sometimes produced naturally when trifluralin is formulated into commercial pesticide products, and the EPA decided to permit the nitrosamine level to double during processing. This means that the cancer risk is two and a half times greater than reported in the final position document used as the basis for completing the special review.

Yet, the product has been labeled safe: the cancer risks associated with it are considered acceptable given its benefits. Health effects tests on trifluralin's potential to cause birth defects, reproduction impairment, mutations, and ecological effects are still required by the EPA, but they will take years to complete. If these tests reveal problems, the EPA may order another Special Review, but meanwhile, the chemical remains on the market.

The final procedural loophole through which the public and the environment may be exposed to dangerous pesticides occurs under the category of special needs and exemptions. Congress permitted the EPA to exempt state and federal agencies from normal registration procedures and requirements when serious pest outbreaks occur for which there are no effective registered pesticides. States may also grant registration for pesticides for a special local need, SLN; that is, for a new and different use other than those for which the pesticide is registered.

Because these emergency and SLN registrations do not include additional requirements for health effects testing, the process is much less burdensome than the regular registration procedures. These emergency exemptions have become an avenue for newer pesticide products to come on to the market before a thorough scientific

THE SAFETY OF PESTICIDES

evaluation is completed under normal procedures. Farmers, farm organizations, government agencies, or pesticide producers can request SLN exemptions, but a study by the Rural Advancement Fund in North Carolina found that between 1978 and 1982 half of the 2,089 SLNs granted in twenty-five states were for use on livestock, forests, and on extensively planted crops including soybeans, small grains, cotton, alfalfa, and corn—the kinds of needs for which special local need is questionable. Ninety-one percent of the SLN registrations granted in these states were requested by the chemical manufacturer, and only 2 percent by farmers and farm organizations.[3]

In summary, farmers, farm workers, and the general public are not yet adequately protected by the present EPA procedures concerning pesticide regulation. Better protection will only come if and when we let our legislators know we want these regulatory procedures strengthened and improved, and that we want the EPA to have the funding and legal clout necessary to carry out its mandate to protect the health of citizens and the long-term viability of our environment.

---

1. General Accounting Office, *Environmental Protection: Agenda for the 1980s,* CED-82-73, May 5, 1982.

2. *Regulatory Procedures and Public Health Issues in the EPA's Office of Pesticide Programs*, Staff Report prepared for the Department of Pesticide Operations, Research, and Foreign Agriculture Subcommittee, House Committee on Agriculture, December 1982.

3. Spalt, Allen, "A Report on 'Special Local Need' Pesticide Registrations, Section 24(c) of FIFRA," Rural Advancement Fund of the National Sharecroppers Fund, July 27, 1983.

The Question of Inerts

The following material was drawn from an article by Mary O'Brien in the Summer 1986 issue of the Journal of Pesticide Reform, *published by the Northwest Coalition for Alternatives to Pesticides. Ms. O'Brien is the editor of the* Journal *and staff scientist for the Coalition. For the purposes of this book her article has been condensed and paraphrased, but all the research work is hers.*

PESTICIDES essentially contain two types of ingredients: "active ingredients"—those listed on the label which are supposed to kill targeted organisms, such as insects, fungi, or mammals—and "inert ingredients", which are those not listed on the label. Inert ingredients can be emulsifiers, solvents, preservatives, antivolatility agents, and contaminants, which are unintended by-products of the manufacturing process. Testing of pesticides for chronic toxicity including cancer, reproductive effects, birth defects, and chronic damage to nerves, kidney, and liver, etc., is required only for active ingredients. The whole issue of pesticide toxicity and safety has been thrown into question because inerts have not been considered—not only for their own potential toxicity, but also for toxicity in combination with the active ingredients.

"Inert" does not mean literally inert, that is, not having active properties, or chemically or biologically inactive. Indeed, some chemicals currently used as inerts are well-known toxins, such as benzene, pentachlorophenol, carbon tetrachloride, asbestos, formaldehyde, xylene, and hexachlorophene, which contains TCDD, or dioxin. The percentage of inert ingredient varies with the type of pesticide. Herbicides often are composed of 50 percent inerts; insecticides often contain more than 50 percent inerts, and some, such as Tordon 2K pellets, are composed of 97 percent inert ingredients.

Approximately 1,200 chemicals have been registered as inert ingredients in 45,000 pesticide formulations. Of these, 55 are known to the Environmental Protection Agency (EPA) to be toxicologically significant. An inert is considered "toxicologically significant" when it has been shown in peer-reviewed studies to cause cancer, nerve damage, or other adverse reproductive or chronic effects. The 55 toxicologically significant inerts "serve largely as solvents or preservatives in formulations. Many contain benzene rings, or toxic metals, or they are halogenated hydrocarbons."[1] About 275 inerts are considered to be harmless, and the toxicity of the remaining 700 to 800 is unknown, although at least 50 are structurally similar to "chemicals with demonstrated health or ecological effects."[2]

Even the manufacturer who registers a pesticide may not know what ingredients are in that pesticide. Pesticide manufacturers are allowed to buy inerts from an inert manufacturer and to send the names of the inerts in an unopened envelope to the EPA. Even the EPA may not know what inerts are in a pesticide for two reasons: first, much of the information on file does not identify the exact chemical makeup of the inerts or actives or important impurities; and second, during the 1972 petroleum shortage, the EPA allowed registrants to purchase scarce solvents and emulsifiers and declare alternatives in their statements of formula. Even if the inert ingredients are known to the manufacturer and EPA, they are not listed on the product and the public is not allowed to know them because inert ingredients have been given trade secret status.

About 600 inert ingredients, including some banned pesticides and chemicals of toxicological concern, have been cleared for use on food or on surfaces that food contacts. Inerts cleared for food are generally exempted from tolerance levels, which means they can legally be found on food in any amount.

Benzene, for example, has been cleared for use on food, in spite of the fact that it is a known human carcinogen which bioaccumulates in the bodies of organisms and was earlier voluntarily cancelled as an active ingredient in pesticides.[3]

Another inert cancelled as an active ingredient but allowed to be used on food is carbon tetrachloride, which is a depressant of the central nervous system, a carcinogen, and a potential groundwater contaminant.[4] Hexachlorophene, a neurotoxin that contains TCDD or dioxin as a contaminant, is a third example of an inert cleared for use on food.[5] Kelthane, or dicofol, used on citrus, pears, and tomatoes, has DDT as one of its inerts, banned as an active ingredient in 1972 because of its damage to wildlife reproduction and its bioaccumulation in organisms.[6]

The EPA recently began to require chemical companies to submit acute toxicity information for the full pesticide formulation on new products. The disadvantages of this requirement are that it applies only to new products, and that the chronic effects of the inert ingredients alone may never be known. The EPA is planning to require minimal testing on the 55 priority inerts, but there are no plans to test the 700 to 800 inerts whose toxicity is unknown.

Meanwhile, when people or other animals or the environment are damaged by exposure to a pesticide, it is impossible to understand what caused that damage unless all the chemicals in the formulation are known. Until these data have been supplied, any quantitative risk analysis of pesticides is meaningless because it has not been based on the full pesticide formulation of active ingredients, intentionally added inert ingredients, and contaminants.

---

1. U.S. Environmental Protection Agency memorandum from John W. Melone, Director, Hazard Evaluation Division, to Phil Gray, Executive Secretary, FIFRA Scientific Advisory Panel, February 11, 1984. Criteria for determining which inert ingredients are of toxicological concern and should be given priority review.

2. Ibid.

3. U.S. Environmental Protection Agency list of inerts of toxicological concern in pesticide products, released June 21, 1985.

4. Ibid.

5. Ibid.

6. U.S. Environmental Protection Agency Proposed Notice of Intent to Cancel Registration of Pesticide Products Containing Dicofol, October 10, 1984. *Federal Register* 49(197):39820-39828.

Pesticides Commonly Found in Foods

THE FOLLOWING table presents only the most commonly detected pesticides in the most commonly consumed fresh fruits and vegetables, and their hazards known to date. It does not cover canned fruit and vegetables, meat, milk, or grains, or all the pesticides used on lawns, in homes, or in industry.

This table is a compilation of material found in *Pesticide Alert* by Lawrie Mott and Karen Snyder of the Natural Resources Defense Council, published by Sierra Club Books. To it I have added material, where available, on pesticide persistence and toxicity to other forms of life as measured by the scale used by the U.S. Council on Environmental Quality. In this scale, nonpersistent implies that the pesticide lasts from a few hours to several days, but not more than twelve weeks; moderately persistent implies that it lasts from one to eighteen months; persistent implies that it lasts for many years—perhaps fifty to one hundred—before degrading. Permanent implies nondegradable, and refers to such elements as mercury, lead, and arsenic.

The information on persistence is from the Environmental Protection Agency's "Pesticide Fact Sheets" and from "Pesticides in Contract Lawn Maintenance," by Ellen M. Rainer and Cynthia T. French, published by the Rachel Carson Council. Where there is no information in a column, it means that I was unable to find information about it, rather than the chemical has no effect.

The produce tested was grown in both the United States and abroad. The data were drawn from the federal government's and California's Department of Food and Agriculture pesticide residue monitoring programs. California's results were included because that state provides the nation with 51 percent of its fresh vegetables and an important percentage of its fresh fruit, and because the FDA does not extensively sample California food in order not to duplicate the state's program.

This table does not present a complete picture, however, because *only the most commonly detected pesticides are listed*, and because both the state and federal standard laboratory tests cannot detect about half the pesticides used on food.

While most of the pesticides detected in these foods occurred in amounts below the tolerances established by EPA, many EPA tolerance levels were established without adequate health and safety data, or by relying on inaccurate assumptions about the volume of fruits and vegetables consumed in the average diet.

Many experts believe that with some health hazards, and especially those involving carcinogens, *any* exposure may be hazardous. There may be no minimum threshold below which exposure is safe. In a letter written to Congressman James D. Florio on November 8, 1983, former EPA Administrator William Ruckelshaus agreed with this position when he wrote: "the Agency is assuming a no-threshold approach for regulating carcinogens." The Delaney clause under Title 21 of the Food and Drugs Code prohibits the use of cancer-causing food additives in any amount, yet the same law allows the presence of carcinogenic pesticides in food.

PESTICIDE **Pesticides in bold type are especially hazardous.** Examples of trade or brand names containing this chemical are shown in parenthesis.	EPA registration date	Use	Commonly consumed produce in which residues are most *commonly* found. These pesticides may be found in other produce, but not as consistently.
Acephate (Orthene)	1972	Insecticide	Bell peppers, celery, green beans, corn
Aldicarb (Temik)	1970	Insecticide	Potatoes, watermelon
Azinphos-methyl (Guthion)	1956	Insecticide	Apples, pears
BHC (HCH, 666, Hexaclor)	1963	Insecticide	Cabbage, sweet potatoes
Captan (Merpan, Orthocide)	1951	Fungicide	Apples, cherries, grapes, peaches, strawberries, watermelon

Whether residues can be reduced by washing, cooking, or heat processing .	Potential health hazards known to date to humans of the pesticide and its contaminants—the unintended byproducts of the manufacturing process.	Potential adverse effects on nontarget species.	Persistence in the environment.
Probably cannot be reduced by washing as residues are systemic. Cooking or heat processing may reduce residues.	Carcinogen for animals and possibly humans. Mutagenic effects in some laboratory test systems. One animal study showed reproductive toxicity.	Birds: medium to high, may affect behavior and breeding success; fish: low; bees: high; plants: low.	Nonpersistent.
Probably cannot be reduced by washing as residues are systemic. Cooking or heat processing may reduce residues.	Toxic at very small doses. Some evidence that it causes changes in human immune system. In 1984 EPA initiated Special Review due to its acute toxicity and the presence of residues in food.	Aldicarb is highly toxic to mammals, birds, estuarine/marine and freshwater organisms. Its residues have contaminated drinking water wells in ten states.	Available data are insufficient to assess its environmental impact.
Residues remain primarily on produce surface and may be reduced by washing, cooking, and heat processing.	Studies are being reviewed by EPA to fill previous data gaps for carcinogenicity, birth defects, reproductive toxicity, and mutagenic effects.	Highly toxic to birds and freshwater fish and other aquatic organisms.	Available data are insufficient to assess its environmental impact.
While residues remain primarily on the produce surface, it is not known if they can be removed with water.	Animal carcinogen. In test animals there is some evidence of male reproductive toxicity.		In 1978 EPA cancelled all uses in the U.S. due to its carcinogenicity, but residues persist in the environment.
Residues remain primarily on the produce surface and may be reduced with washing, cooking, and heat processing. However, one of its metabolites or breakdown products, THPI, may be systemic; it is a suspected carcinogen.	Probable human carcinogen. Laboratory tests showed some evidence of mutagenic effects. In 1980 EPA initiated a Special Review due to its carcinogenicity, mutagenic effects, and the presence of its residues in foods.	Birds: low to medium; fish: very high; earthworms: high; bees: if taken in orally—high; on its epidermis—low; damages bee larvae; plants: increased incidence of gall in cherry trees.	Nonpersistent to moderately persistent.

PESTICIDE **Pesticides in bold type are especially hazardous.** Examples of trade or brand names containing this chemical are shown in parenthesis.	EPA registration date	Use	Commonly consumed produce in which residues are most *commonly* found. These pesticides may be found in other produce, but not as consistently.
Carbaryl (Sevin)	1958	Insecticide, herbicide, synergist	Bananas, corn, grapefruit, grapes, oranges, peaches, watermelon
Chlordane (Octachlor, Velsicol 1068)	1948	Insecticide	Potatoes
Chlorobenzilate (Acaraben)	1953	Insecticide	Grapefruit
Chloropropham (CIPC)	1962	Herbicide	Potatoes

Whether residues can be reduced by washing, cooking, or heat processing.	Potential health hazards known to date to humans of the pesticide and its contaminants—the unintended byproducts of the manufacturing process.	Potential adverse effects on nontarget species.	Persistence in the environment.
Residues remain primarily on the produce surface and may be reduced by washing and peeling.	In humans there is some evidence of adverse kidney effects, and mutagenic effects in laboratory tests. In animal studies there was no observed carcinogenicity or reproductive toxicity.	Birds: low to high; fish: medium to very high; crustaceans: high to very high; mollusks: medium to high; earthworms: very high; bees: very high; aquatic insects: very high; aquatic worms: medium to high; plants: toxic to some.	Nonpersistent to moderately persistent.
Residues remain primarily on the produce surface, although in root crops there is some evidence that they are systemic. It is not known whether residues can be removed with water.	Probable human carcinogen. Laboratory studies reveal some evidence of birth defects, reproductive toxicity, and mutagenic effects. Agricultural uses were cancelled by EPA in 1978.	Highly toxic to birds and aquatic organisms.	Its residues persist in the environment and in body tissues. In 1987 EPA cancelled interior home use to control termites. Available data are insufficient to assess the environmental impact of chlordane.
Residues remain primarily on the citrus peel; washing and processing will reduce them.	Animal carcinogen. Some evidence of reproductive toxicity, including adverse testicular effects in test animals. One of its contaminants is DDT. In 1979 EPA cancelled all uses in the U.S. *except* on citrus, due to its carcinogenicity and reproductive toxicity.		Available data are insufficient to assess the enviromental impact of chlorobenzilate.
Residues are primarily systemic and probably cannot be reduced by washing.	Has not been sufficiently tested for cancer; some evidence of mutagenic effects in laboratory tests.	Moderately toxic to freshwater fish.	Available data are insufficient to assess its environmental impact.

PESTICIDE **Pesticides in bold type are especially hazardous.** Examples of trade or brand names containing this chemical are shown in parenthesis.	EPA registration date	Use	Commonly consumed produce in which residues are most *commonly* found. These pesticides may be found in other produce, but not as consistently.
Chlorothalonil (Bravo)	1966	Fungicide	Cantaloupes, cauliflower, celery, green beans, tomatoes, watermelon
Chlorpyrifos (Dursban)	1965	Insecticide	Bell peppers, corn, cucumbers, oranges, tomatoes
Cyhexatin (Plictran)	1972	Insecticide	Pears
DCPA (Dacthal, Chlorthaldimethyl)	1958	Herbicide	Broccoli, onions

Whether residues can be reduced by washing, cooking, or heat processing.	Potential health hazards known to date to humans of the pesticide and its contaminants—the unintended byproducts of the manufacturing process.	Potential adverse effects on nontarget species.	Persistence in the environment.
Residues remain primarily on the produce surface, and may be reduced by washing or cooking. However, chlorothalonil metabolites may be systemic.	Probable human carcinogen. Some evidence of mutagenic and chronic health effects, in the kidney, thyroid, liver, and stomach. No observed birth defects in animal studies. Hexachlorobenzene (HCB), one of its contaminants, is a probable human carcinogen.	Birds: low; fish: very high; bees: low; plants: toxic to some.	Moderately persistent.
Residues remain primarily on produce surface, but it is not known whether they can be removed with water.	According to EPA it has not been sufficiently tested for chronic toxicity, carcinogenicity, or mutagenic effects. It is cumulative.	Birds: high to very high; fish: very high; affects behavior and equilibrium; crustaceans: very high; bees: very high; aquatic insects: very high; plants: toxic to some.	Moderately persistent.
Cyhexatin does not readily dissolve in water; washing may not reduce residues, but peeling may. Residues remain primarily on the produce surface, and are greater in processed foods than in fresh fruits.	In 1987, Dow Chemical and Chevron requested voluntary cancellation of their registration, initiated recalls of all remaining stocks, and halted all production worldwide due to mounting evidence of birth defects in humans.	Causes birth defects and some adverse health effects on the livers of test animals.	Available data are insufficient on the environmental impact of cyhexatin.
Some evidence that residues are systemic, and persistent in the environment. There is no information on whether residues can be removed with water.	According to EPA, it has not been sufficiently tested for carcinogenicity or mutagenic effects. One of its contaminants, hexachlorobenzene, is known to cause cancer; birth defects; fetal toxicity; and bone, eye, heart, kidney, liver, nerve, and thyroid damage.	In birds it causes low breeding success, liver and kidney damage; fish: liver, kidney, and gall bladder damage. It is cumulative in humans and other forms of life.	It is moderately persistent, and one of its contaminants, hexachlorobenzene, is persistent.

PESTICIDE **Pesticides in bold type are especially hazardous.** Examples of trade or brand names containing this chemical are shown in parenthesis.	EPA registration date	Use	Commonly consumed produce in which residues are most *commonly* found. These pesticides may be found in other produce, but not as consistently.
DDT	1945	Insecticide	Carrots, cauliflower, onions, potatoes, spinach, sweet potatoes
Demeton (Systox)	1955	Insecticide	Broccoli
Diazinon (Spectrocide, Sarolex)	1952	Insecticide, nematocide	Bananas, carrots, cauliflower, cherries, onions
Dicloran (DNCA, Botran)	1961	Fungicide	Celery, cherries, grapes, peaches, sweet potatoes

Whether residues can be reduced by washing, cooking, or heat processing.	Potential health hazards known to date to humans of the pesticide and its contaminants—the unintended byproducts of the manufacturing process.	Potential adverse effects on nontarget species.	Persistence in the environment.
Residues remain primarily on the produce surface, although they may be absorbed into the peel. In root crops, washing and peeling will reduce residues but cooking won't.	In 1972 EPA cancelled all uses in the U.S. due to carcinogenicity, bioaccumulation, and other chronic effects.		Persistent.
Residues are systemic and probably cannot be removed by washing.	There is some evidence of birth defects and mutagenic effects in laboratory studies. According to EPA, it has not been sufficiently tested for birth defects, carcinogenicity, reproductive toxicity, or mutagenic effects.	Highly toxic to birds, fish, and freshwater invertebrates.	Available studies are insufficient to determine its environmental impact.
Residues remain primarily on the produce surface. It is not known if they can be removed by washing.	No observed carcinogenicity or reproductive toxicity in animal studies. One of its contaminants, sulfotepp, is a known carcinogen.	Birds: very high; amphibians: low to medium; fish: very high; crustaceans: very high; bees: very high; aquatic insects: very high; plants: toxic to some. It degrades into TEPP, which is highly toxic to all wildlife.	Nonpersistent to moderately persistent.
Residues remain on plant's leaves after foliar treatment, but if the soil has been treated, residues are absorbed and translocated to edible tissue. Residues may be reduced by washing, peeling, cooking, or heat processing. Dicloran is sometimes used in waxes used to maintain the cosmetic appeal of produce; since they cannot be washed off, pesticide residues are sealed into the food.	In one animal study there was no reproductive toxicity observed. According to EPA it has not been sufficiently tested for carcinogenicity, birth defects, or mutagenicity.		Available data are insufficient to assess its environmental impact.

PESTICIDE **Pesticides in bold type are especially hazardous.** Examples of trade or brand names containing this chemical are shown in parenthesis.	EPA registration date	Use	Commonly consumed produce in which residues are most *commonly* found. These pesticides may be found in other produce, but not as consistently.
Dieldrin	1949	Insecticide	Carrots, corn, cucumbers, potatoes, sweet potatoes
Dimethoate (Cygon, Rogon)	1963	Insecticide	Bell peppers, broccoli, cabbage, cantaloupes, cauliflower, cucumbers, grapes, green beans, lettuce, spinach, tomatoes, watermelon
Diphenylamine (DPA)	1962	Plant growth regulator and insecticide	Apples
Endosulfan (Thiodan)	early 1960s	Insecticide	Apples, bell peppers, cantaloupes, cauliflower, celery, cucumbers, green beans, lettuce, peaches, pears, spinach, strawberries
Ethion (Ethanox, Ethiol, Rhodocide)	1972	Insecticide	Grapefruit, onions, oranges, pears

Whether residues can be reduced by washing, cooking, or heat processing.	Potential health hazards known to date to humans of the pesticide and its contaminants—the unintended byproducts of the manufacturing process.	Potential adverse effects on nontarget species.	Persistence in the environment.
Residues remain primarily on the produce surface, although in root crops there is some evidence that they may be systemic. Peeling or cooking may reduce residues, but it is not known if they can be removed with water.	Probable human carcinogen. In animal studies it also causes birth defects and reproductive toxicity. Low levels reduced learning capabilities in monkeys.		In 1974, EPA cancelled all uses in the U.S. due to its carcinogenicity, bioaccumulation, and other chronic effects. It may still be detectable in crops due to its persistence in the soil, illegal use, or use in foreign countries where it is not banned.
Residues are systemic; yet they were reduced by washing, peeling, cooking, or heat processing in several studies.	Laboratory studies have shown some evidence of carcinogenicity, birth defects, reproductive toxicity, and mutagenic effects.	Has caused mutations in fungi, bacteria, plants, and mice.	Available data are insufficient to assess its environmental impact.
Residues remain primarily in the peel. Diphenylamine does not easily dissolve in water; therefore washing with water may not reduce residues but peeling may.	Animal studies have revealed some evidence of adverse kidney and blood effects. According to EPA, it has not been sufficiently tested for long-term health effects.		Available data are insufficient to assess its environmental impact.
Residues remain primarily on the produce surface; however, endosulfan breakdown products may be systemic. There is no information on whether they can be removed with water. Peeling, cooking, or heat processing may slightly reduce residues.	There is some evidence of adverse chronic effects including liver and kidney damage, and testicular atrophy in test animals. There was no observed mutagenic effects in laboratory tests.		Available data are insufficient to assess its environmental impact.
Residues remain primarily on the produce surface. Washing or processing may reduce them.	Studies are being reviewed by EPA to fill data gaps on carcinogenicity, birth defects, mutagenicity, and reproductive toxicity.		Available data are insufficient to assess its environmental impact.

219

PESTICIDE **Pesticides in bold type are especially hazardous.** Examples of trade or brand names containing this chemical are shown in parenthesis.	EPA registration date	Use	Commonly consumed produce in which residues are most *commonly* found. These pesticides may be found in other produce, but not as consistently.
Fenvalerate (Pydrin, Belmark)	1979	Insecticide	Cabbage
Iprodione (Rovral)	1980	Fungicide	Grapes
Lindane (Agronexit, Lindafor, Gamma BHC)	1950	Insecticide	Corn
Malathion (Cythion)	1950s	Insecticide	Cantaloupes, cherries, onions
Methamidophos (Monitor)	1972	Insecticide	Bell peppers, broccoli, cabbage, cantaloupes, cauliflower, celery, cucumbers, green beans, spinach, strawberries, tomatoes, watermelon

Whether residues can be reduced by washing, cooking, or heat processing.	Potential health hazards known to date to humans of the pesticide and its contaminants—the unintended byproducts of the manufacturing process.	Potential adverse effects on nontarget species.	Persistence in the environment.
Residues remain primarily on the produce surface, but fenvalerate does not easily dissolve in water, so washing may not reduce residues.	There is some evidence of carcinogenicity in the only available studies. Laboratory studies produced no observed birth defects, reproductive toxicity, or mutagenic effects.	Toxic to wildlife; extremely toxic to fish.	Available data are insufficient to assess its environmental impact.
Residues remain primarily on the produce surface, but there is no information on whether they can be removed with water.	There is some evidence of adverse health effects including liver, urinary, and immune system damage, and mutagenic effects in laboratory studies. There were no observed birth defects in animal studies.	Birds: low to medium.	Available data are insufficient to assess its environmental impact.
There is some evidence that residues are systemic. It is not known whether they can be removed with water.	Lindane is a possible human carcinogen. Its chronic effects include blood disorders (aplastic anemia) and liver and kidney damage in test animals.	Toxic to fish and aquatic invertebrates.	Available data are insufficient to assess its enviromental impact.
Residues remain primarily on the produce surface, but may be absorbed into the peel. Peeling, cooking, or heat processing will reduce residues. Washing with detergent is more effective than washing with plain water.	There is some evidence of reproductive toxicity in the only available animal study. There were no observed mutagenic effects in available laboratory studies.	Birds: medium; amphibians: medium to very high; fish and crustaceans: medium to very high; earthworms: high; bees: very high; aquatic insects: very high; aquatic worms: medium.	Nonpersistent.
Residues are systemic and probably cannot be removed with washing.	EPA is reviewing studies submitted to fill previous data gaps for carcinogenicity, birth defects, reproductive toxicity, and mutagenic effects.		Available data are insufficient to assess its environmental impact.

PESTICIDE **Pesticides in bold type are especially hazardous.** Examples of trade or brand names containing this chemical are shown in parenthesis.	EPA registration date	Use	Commonly consumed produce in which residues are most *commonly* found. These pesticides may be found in other produce, but not as consistently.
Methidathion (Supracide, Somonil)	1972	Insecticide	Grapefruit, oranges
Methomyl (Lannate)	1963	Insecticide	Celery, lettuce, spinach
Methyl Parathion (Folidol M, Metacide)	1954	Insecticide	Strawberries, cantaloupes
Mevinphos (Phosdrin)	1958	Insecticide	Lettuce

Whether residues can be reduced by washing, cooking, or heat processing.	Potential health hazards known to date to humans of the pesticide and its contaminants—the unintended byproducts of the manufacturing process.	Potential adverse effects on nontarget species.	Persistence in the environment.
Residues remain primarily on the citrus peel. It is not known whether water will remove them.	There is some evidence of carcinogenicity in animal studies, but no observed mutagenic effects in laboratory test systems. According to EPA, it has not been sufficiently tested for carcinogenicity, birth defects, or reproductive toxicity.	Discernible chronic health effects in animals.	Available data are insufficient to assess its environmental impact.
Residues are systemic and probably cannot be removed with washing.	Animal studies have shown some evidence of mutagenic effects and adverse chronic health effects including kidney, spleen, and blood changes, but no observed carcinogenicity, birth defects, or reproductive toxicity. Acetamide, one of its metabolites or breakdown products, is a possible human carcinogen.	Bees: high.	Available data are insufficient to assess its environmental impact.
Residues remain primarily on the produce surface, but there is some evidence that they can be absorbed. It is not known whether residues can be removed with water.	There is some evidence of carcinogenicity and adverse chronic health effects including blood changes in animal studies and mutagenic effects. According to EPA, it has not been sufficiently tested for carcinogenicity or birth defects.	Highly toxic to humans, laboratory mammals, birds, and aquatic invertebrates. Poses a hazard to many endangered species.	Available data are insufficient to assess its environmental impact.
Residues are systemic and probably cannot be removed with washing.	According to EPA, it has not been sufficiently tested for acute toxicity, subchronic effects, carcinogenicity, reproductive effects, mutagenicity, and metabolic effects.	Highly toxic to humans, aquatic organisms, and birds. Jeopardizes endangered species.	Available data are insufficient to assess its enviromental impact.

PESTICIDE **Pesticides in bold type are especially hazardous.** Examples of trade or brand names containing this chemical are shown in parenthesis.	EPA registration date	Use	Commonly consumed produce in which residues are most *commonly* found. These pesticides may be found in other produce, but not as consistently.
Parathion (Phoskil)	1948	Insecticide	Bell peppers, broccoli, carrots, cherries, oranges, peaches
Permethrin (Ambush, Pounce)	1978	Insecticide	Cabbage, lettuce, tomatoes
Phosmet (Imidan)	1966	Insecticide	Apples, pears, sweet potatoes
Sulfallate (CDEC, Vegadex)	1973	Herbicide	Corn
Thiabendazole (TBZ, Mertect)	1968	Fungicide, nematocide	Bananas, grapefruit

Whether residues can be reduced by washing, cooking, or heat processing.	Potential health hazards known to date to humans of the pesticide and its contaminants—the unintended byproducts of the manufacturing process.	Potential adverse effects on nontarget species.	Persistence in the environment.
Residues remain primarily on the produce surface, and washing, peeling, cooking, or heat processing may slightly reduce them.	It is a possible human carcinogen. There is some evidence of retinal and sciatic nerve degeneration. It is now under Special Review because of its acute effects on both humans and birds.	Extremely toxic to laboratory animals, fish, and birds.	Available data are insufficient to assess its environmental impact.
Residues remain primarily on the produce surface; plain water may not reduce residues, but washing with detergent will.	It is a possible human carcinogen. There is some evidence of reproductive toxicity in one animal study, but no observed birth defects or mutagenic effects in laboratory studies.	Bees: high; fish: high.	Available data are insufficient to assess its environmental impact.
Residues remain primarily on the produce surface and washing or cooking will reduce them.	It is a possible human carcinogen. There is some evidence of mutagenic effects in laboratory test systems and pesticide factory workers; additional mutagenic studies are required.	Highly toxic to honeybees, fish, aquatic and estuarine invertebrates. Mildly toxic to mammals and slightly toxic to birds.	Available data are insufficient to assess its environmental impact.
Sulfallate is readily absorbed by roots and from there throughout the plant. It is not absorbed by foliage. It is not known whether it can be removed with water.	There is some evidence of carcinogenicity and mutagenic effects in laboratory studies. In 1981 production was discontinued in the U.S.		Available data are insufficient to assess its environmental impact.
Residues remain primarily on the peel and are reduced by peeling or washing. If it has been used as a wax additive, it can't be washed off.	There are no observed carcinogenicity or birth defects in test animals.	Earthworms: high.	Persistent.

PESTICIDE **Pesticides in bold type are especially hazardous.** Examples of trade or brand names containing this chemical are shown in parenthesis.	EPA registration date	Use	Commonly consumed produce in which residues are most *commonly* found. These pesticides may be found in other produce, but not as consistently.
Trifluralin (Treflan)	1963	Herbicide	Carrots
Vinclozolin (Ronilan)	1981	Fungicide	Strawberries

Whether residues can be reduced by washing, cooking, or heat processing.	Potential health hazards known to date to humans of the pesticide and its contaminants—the unintended byproducts of the manufacturing process.	Potential adverse effects on nontarget species.	Persistence in the environment.
Residues are systemic and probably cannot be reduced with washing, particularly in root crops. Peeling may reduce residues in carrots.	It is a possible human carcinogen. There is some evidence of adverse health effects including kidney changes in test animals. There were no observed birth defects, reproductive toxicity, or mutagenic effects in laboratory studies. However, its contaminants are nitrosamines, some of which are carcinogens.	Birds: low; amphibians: very high; fish: low to very high; crustaceans: high to very high; bees: low to medium; aquatic insects: high.	Moderately persistent.
Residues remain primarily on the produce surface, but there is some evidence that they can be absorbed. They can be reduced by cooking or heat processing.	There was some evidence of mutagenic effects in one laboratory test system, but no observed birth defects in available animal studies.		Available data are insufficient to assess its environmental impact.

At Green Gulch Farm strawberry baskets become miniature greenhouses, protecting seedlings from the sun, wind, and birds.

Pesticide Resources

ORGANIZATIONS WORKING TO PROTECT OUR ENVIRONMENT

National Coalition Against the Misuse of Pesticides
530 Seventh St. S.E.
Washington, D.C. 20003
1-202-543-5450

NCAMP is a nonprofit membership organization committed to pesticide safety for both humans and the environment. It promotes the adoption of alternative pest management strategies which reduce or eliminate a dependency on toxic chemicals. It maintains an extensive file of toxicological literature on pesticides and provides summaries of published data and information on which pesticides have not been fully tested for health hazards. One year's membership for an individual is $20.00.

National Pesticide Telecommunications Network
1-800-858-7378

The number above is a 24-hour "Pesticide Hotline" funded by the U.S. Environmental Protection Agency and Texas Tech University. It provides information on pesticide toxicity and proper use of pesticides. For more information on the services of this network write:

NPTN
Texas Tech University
Health Sciences Center
School of Medicine, Department of Preventive
    Medicine
Lubbock, Texas 79430

The Rachel Carson Council
8940 Jones Mill Road
Chevy Chase, MD 20815
1-301-652-1877

RCC was founded in 1965 to carry out Rachel
Carson's wish for an independent, objective
information center on the environmental and
human health effects of toxic chemical
contamination, especially from pesticides.

Americans for Safe Food
1501 Sixteenth St., N.W.
Washington, D.C. 20036
1-202-332-9110

ASF, part of the Center for Science in the
Public Interest, is a coalition of more than
eighty environmental and farm groups
working to increase the availability of safer
food in the marketplace.

**Northwest Coalition for Alternatives to
    Pesticides**
P.O. Box 1393
Eugene, Oregon 97440
1-503-344-5044

NCAP was started in 1977 to challenge the
aerial spraying of herbicides over public
forests in the Northwest. It expanded to
represent citizens and organizations in five
states; today more than half of the requests it
receives for information come from all over the
country. It challenges pesticide dependence in
forest, agricultural, roadside, aquatic, and
urban settings, and publishes the quarterly
Journal of Pesticide Reform. The *Journal's* yearly
cost for an individual is $15.00.

Mothers and Others for Pesticide Limits
c/o National Resources Defense Council
P.O. Box 96641
Washington, D.C. 20090
1-202-783-7800

The legal amounts or tolerances of pesticides
allowed by the EPA in foods are based on
estimated *adult* consumption. This
organization's concern is that these guidelines
do not take children's increased susceptibility
to carcinogens into account. Their developing
brains and nervous systems are more sensitive
to damage, and children also retain more
pesticides in their bodies. They have a more
permeable gastrointestinal tract and do not
excrete toxins from the body as easily as
adults. This organization publishes a book, *For
Our Kids' Sake: How to Protect Your Children
From Pesticides in Food*, which is available from
them for $7.95.

Bio-Integral Resource Center
P.O. Box 7414
Berkeley, CA 94707
1-415-524-2567

BIRC is a nonprofit organization founded in
1978 to publish practical information on the
least toxic methods of managing plant diseases
and insect, weed, and rodent pests. On a
monthly basis, BIRC's technical staff scans the
world's scientific literature for the least toxic
methods of controlling pests in agriculture,
urban landscapes and structures, greenhouses,
nurseries, forestry, medical, veterinary, range,
and other settings.

It publishes *The Common Sense Pest Control
Quarterly* for nontechnical readers such as
homeowners and gardeners, and *The IPM
Quarterly*, an international monthly newsletter
on Integrated Pest Management for
professionals in agriculture, forestry, ranching,
and urban settings. BIRC's technical staff has
over eighteen years' experience in designing
and implementing IPM programs for public
agencies and private businesses in the U.S.

and Canada. For a publications catalog and further information on membership, send a self-addressed business envelope and $1.00 to cover postage and handling.

Rodale Press and Research Center
33 E. Minor Street
Emmaus, PA 18098
1-215-967-5171

In addition to *Organic Gardening* and *Prevention* magazines, The Rodale Center publishes *New Farmer*, the only farming magazine in the world specializing in low input farming methods.

The Land Institute
2440 East Water Well Road
Salina, Kansas 67401
1-913-823-5376

A private, nonprofit research and education center devoted to sustainable agriculture.

National Coalition to Stop Food Irradiation
P.O. Box 59-0488
San Francisco, CA 94159
1-415-626-2734

A nonprofit citizens group created to inform the public about the dangers of irradiated food.

Old bedsprings find a new use as a garden trellis for beans in the Ala Wai Community Garden, Honolulu, Hawaii.

Community Garden Resources

A community garden is a portion of land that has been divided into plots and is cultivated either individually or communally. On the North American continent, Native Americans cultivated food communally for centuries. When the Pilgrims first arrived, they too adopted a communal way of growing food, but as settlements became more spread out, they began to farm independently.

Community gardens are an excellent way for city dwellers to enjoy the pleasures of gardening; they are often sponsored by park departments, churches, horticultural groups, businesses, helping agencies, and individuals.

To find out more about gardens in your area or how to start one, contact these groups:

The Cooperative Extension Service is a government organization that provides gardeners with publications, information on local gardening problems and needs, soil testing, and project support. It is part of the Agricultural Extension Service, and there is an office in every county of every state. It is listed in phone directories under "Cooperative Extension" or "Extension," or under the name of your county.

231

The American Community Gardening Association
P.O. Box 400
Glencoe, Illinois 60022

ACGA is a national nonprofit organization of two hundred professional garden organizers dedicated to improving communities through horticulture. Its regional directors can provide technical assistance to community garden projects in their area.

National Gardening Association
180 Flynn Ave.
Burlington, VT 05401
1-802-863-1308

The National Gardening Association publishes *The Community Garden Book*, by Larry Sommers, a practical, hands-on guide to the creation and maintenance of community garden projects. It explores successful community garden projects and includes excellent information on locating sponsors, fund raising, site design, soil care, and dealing with problems of vandalism. Its cost is $10.95 including postage.

Most of the National Gardening Association's programs are geared for children. The National Gardening Grants program provides material and instructional support for childrens' gardening programs. *The National Association's Guide to Kid's Garden Projects*, by Lynn Ocone with Eve Pranis, is also published by the Association. It tells how to start and manage gardening projects with children, and includes seventy-five low-cost or no-cost learning activities. Its cost is $12.95 including UPS shipping.

"Grow Lab" is a school science program for kindergarten through eighth grade. The curriculum was developed with a grant from the National Science Foundation; it teaches science and math through gardening, and is currently being used in over 4,000 schools. For more information contact the Association.

More of Marcia Donahue's mythological figures spring from the soil as naturally as plants.

Glossary

Acid soil: Soil without lime. Acid soils tend to breed bacteria more slowly than alkaline soils; they often have a spongy, loose texture but fertility is limited. A factor causing acidity is rainfall which carries sulfuric acid gathered from the air as it falls. The addition of limestone corrects acid soil. Acidity is measured by the pH scale, which counts the number of hydrogen ions. The neutral point on the scale is 7. Soil testing below pH 7 is acid; soil testing above pH 7 is alkaline.

Actinomycetes: Bacteria which are important in the breakdown of decaying organic material and are responsible for moldy odor.

Alkaline soil: The soils of deserts and rainless places. The addition of ground agricultural sulfur corrects alkaline soil.

Alpine: A native plant found in the mountains which flowers in spring, soon after the snow melts. When used by gardeners, the term can refer to any plant small enough to be grown in a rock garden.

Annual: A plant whose entire life span—from seed to flowering to death—occurs within a year or less.

Bacteria: Single-celled microorganisms which help break down plant and animal tissues in soil so that nutrients become available for absorption by plant roots. Bacteria may also cause plant diseases.

Bed: A plot for flowers or vegetables in the center of a garden, as opposed to a border, which goes around the periphery of a garden.

Bedding plants: Annuals or biennials which are put in place for one season only, then dug up and removed. Since they use nutrients in the soil without returning anything to it, the areas where they grow have to be constantly fertilized and renewed.

Biennial: A plant that lives for two seasons, producing leaves the first year and flowering and seeding before dying in the second.

Biodynamic: A term first coined in 1924 to describe Rudolf Steiner's view of agriculture, based on an understanding of the interrelationships of living organisms and ecological processes and Steiner's spiritual views. In the United States, the term *biodynamic* often implies a method of growing based on ecological principles without a formalized spiritual base.

Bloom, Alan: (1906-) A widely known British nurseryman and author who specializes in herbaceous perennials and alpines.

Blow sand: Loose sand, blown from a distance, containing little organic matter.

Bog plants: Plants adapted to living in permanently wet soil; their roots take in oxygen from water rather than aerated soil.

Bolting: The premature production of flowers often caused by hot, dry weather, inadequate watering, or starvation.

Bonemeal: Organic fertilizer made from pulverized animal bones. It provides a good source of phosphate and a small source of nitrogen.

Border plants: Generally refers to herbaceous or hardy perennials.

Burbank, Luther: (1849-1926) A famous North American horticulturist who introduced and developed many new fruits, flowers, and grasses. He is most famous for the Burbank potato, the Santa Rosa plum, and the Shasta daisy.

Chadwick, Alan: (1910-1980) A Shakespearean actor and horticulturist who combined Rudolf Steiner's biodynamics with the French intensive method of horticulture. He inspired thousands of students to garden while teaching at various gardens in California and in Virginia. His most extensive project was at University of California's Santa Cruz campus.

Chemically grown: Plants grown with the aid of commercial fertilizers, pesticides, and herbicides.

Combine: A harvesting machine that not only cuts the plant but also separates the grains from the leaves and stalks.

Commercial fertilizers: Chemical compounds derived through industrial processing, available in liquid or granular forms.

Compost: Decomposed vegetable matter that contains not only the major elements for healthy plant growth, but trace minerals as well. Compost enriches the soil and increases its ability to hold water.

Cutting: A stem, root, or leaf which, when removed from its parent plant and properly cultivated, will produce a complete new plant.

Double-digging: Turning over the soil to a depth of two spades. Loosening the soil to this depth allows easy root and water penetration.

Fibonacci phyllotaxis or series: A method for analyzing leaf arrangements by expressing mathematically as a fraction the angle of divergence between two successive leaves, e.g., 1/2, 1/3, 2/5, etc., in which each succeeding fraction is the sum of the two previous numerators and the sum of the two previous denominators.

Flints: (*Zea mays indurata*) A class of corn with kernels that are soft and starchy in the center but enclosed by a hard outer layer. They are usually used in animal feed.

Foliar spray: A solution of fertilizer and water sprayed directly on the foliage of plants, where it is quickly absorbed.

French intensive method: Growing techniques, such as raised beds and closely spaced planting, that produced large harvests from small lots in the 18th and 19th century market gardens of France. Up to nine crops were obtained annually from the same bed through a complicated process of staged interplantings and careful soil amendment and fertilization.

Fungicide: A chemical that kills fungi or prevents their growth.

Genus: A category of classification between family and species; a group of structurally or phylogenetically related species, or an isolated species exhibiting unusual differentiation. The first word of the scientific name of a species is the genus name, and is capitalized.

Grain binder: A harvesting machine rarely seen today. It not only cut the grain stalks but also bound them in bundles. The bundles were then stacked by hand to dry, and when dry, run through a threshing machine.

Green manure: A crop of growing plants that is plowed under while still green to decay in and thereby enrich the soil.

Hardpan soil: An impervious layer of soil lying at or beneath the surface through which roots and water cannot penetrate.

Heirloom varieties: Older open-pollinated seeds or plants that have been saved by generations of gardeners because these seeds or plants had the traits that home gardeners wanted.

Humus: The black or dark brown end product of decaying organic material in the soil.

Hybrid: A plant produced by crossing two different species, true-breeding varieties, or genera.

Jeavons, John: (1942-) A West Coast horticulturalist widely known for developing biodynamic/French intensive methods of food production. These methods have been applied successfully in developing as well as industrialized countries.

Lime: An inorganic substance containing calcium oxide, a chemical that reacts with carbon dioxide in the air and water in the soil to produce carbonate of lime, which neutralizes acids in soils.

Mulch: A layer of material covering the soil that holds moisture in and makes it more difficult for weeds to grow.

Mycorrhiza: Threads of fungus found in a mutually beneficial association with the root cells of many plants and forest trees.

Open-pollinated: Seeds or plants produced through the crossing of the same species; the opposite of hybrid.

Organic fertilizers: Natural materials—such as manure, compost, green manures, bone and blood meal—that nourish the soil slowly as they decay.

Organically grown: Plants grown with the aid of organic fertilizers and natural pest controls.

Pelleted seeds: Very small seeds which are individually coated with a soil-clay mixture to make them easier to plant, thereby reducing waste and the need for thinning.

Perennial: A plant that lives for more than two years. Often applied exclusively to herbaceous perennials, i.e., plants producing stems that die down each year.

Pesticide: A chemical used to kill a targeted pest which kills beneficial organisms as well.

Pinching: Removing new plant growth before it elongates into stems. Pinching out terminal buds makes young plants bushier, while pinching back side growth helps a plant grow taller.

Pricking out: Gently transplanting a seedling out of the soil in which it germinated into a pot, pan, or bed in order to give it more growing space.

Red thread: A disease found in grasses caused by a fungus (*Laetisaria fuciformis*) growing in such a way that it looks like red threads running through the grass.

Salal: (*Gaultheria shallon*) An evergreen shrub that can grow four to ten feet in good soil. It has nearly round, glossy bright green leaves, and white or pinkish bell-like flowers on reddish stalks in loose, six-inch long clusters. Its edible black fruit resemble large huckleberries and have a bland flavor liked by birds.

Scion: A scion or cion is a detached plant shoot with one or more buds that is inserted by grafting into a rootstock, producing the same kind of tree or shrub from which it was taken.

Self-fertile: Able to produce fruit after accepting its own pollen.

Sheet erosion: Erosion that occurs over the entire surface of an area, rather than in isolated valleys.

Soil: Mineral particles surrounded by dead and living organic material, with air spaces in between.

Species: A subdivision of a genus whose member plants are mutually fertile and resemble each other to such an extent that they might have had a common parent.

Sugaries: (*Zea mays saccharata*) Sweet corn, which has kernels that are translucent and more or less wrinkled at maturity, and has a sweet taste because the endosperm contains sugar as well as starch.

Swather: A harvesting machine that functioned somewhat like a giant hedgeclipper, only the stalks were also crushed in the process so that they would dry more evenly. It was used most often to cut hay or grains.

Topdressing: The application of compost, lime, manure, or other fertilizers to the surface of the soil.

Topiary: The art of shaping vines, shrubs, and trees into ornamental shapes.

Vermiculite: A mineral containing mica that, after being processed, is used as a medium for growing plants. When vermiculite ore is heated to 2,000° F, the granules rapidly expand as moisture inside them turns to steam, creating tiny air cells within the mineral which provide room for water and air.

Wind row: Loose piles of cut stalks that allow for more uniform drying. If the stalks were just cut and left flat on the ground, the top side would dry before the bottom side, creating the opportunity for spoilage.

Zones of hardiness: Plant climate zones or areas in which a common set of temperature ranges, humidity patterns, and other geographic and seasonal characteristics combine to allow certain plants to succeed and others to fail.